GRAPPA
THOUGHTS

GRAPPA
THOUGHTS

Bruno Amalia-Manfredi (Bam)

Archway Publishing books may be ordered through booksellers or by contacting:

Archway Publishing
1663 Liberty Drive
Bloomington, IN 47403
www.archwaypublishing.com
844-669-3957

ISBN: 978-1-6657-0836-4 (sc)
ISBN: 978-1-6657-0835-7 (hc)
ISBN: 978-1-6657-0837-1 (e)

Library of Congress Control Number: 2021912268

Print information available on the last page.

Archway Publishing rev. date: 6/30/2021

CONTENTS

INTRODUCTION

Grappa is an Italian spirit that can best be described as a cross between French cognac and American moonshine. The history goes
something like this. In days gone by, the wealthy made wine by
pressing the juice from grapes and then discarding the seeds, skins,
and stems, which the poor took and cooked in a fashion similar to
how moonshine is made resulting in the very potent and delicious
liquor we have come to know as grappa. And just as there are good
wines and shitty-tasting, paint-thinner wines, there are great grappas
and ones that go best with a toilet brush.

Many great writers, musicians, and armchair politicians speak of
how they had some of their greatest epiphanies after a drink or two or
ten or after they just got fucked up on their spirit of choice. What fol-
lows is my version that came to me after many grappa-infused nights
over the years and what (at the time) seemed to be brilliant, noteworthy
insights. Some nights may have been only a couple of shots while other
nights, I was blind-dog drunk in a room with no doors. As many of the
latter nights wore on and more and more was consumed, the insights
did at times become pretty damn hard to decipher, but with the help of
some of my colleagues, we half-assed pieced them together thereafter.

I am what I would consider to be a realist. My beautiful wife
would call me aggressive, while others I'm sure would just say I was
an unfiltered asshole. I tend to call things as I see them, and I'm not
scared to speak my mind. I don't go out looking to hurt anyone or
make someone feel shitty about anything, but I also will not shy away
and hide and hole up when I believe someone is spouting off about
some totally stupid barnyard bullshit.

I am typically more than willing to help anyone truly in need or looking for help, and if sometimes that means punching them figuratively in the throat with a velvet glove to wake them the hell up, so be it. I will however almost always then help them back up. The one exception is if that person looking for help is only going to take my hand up to piss all over my feet. Then simply, fuck 'em.

Stay on your side of the street because if you come in my yard trying to fill your pockets at my or my family's expense with some sad story or just flat-out trying to steal from me, don't expect help from me. Hell, I'm more likely to drop a deuce on you after the proverbial punch and then ever so gently open my back gate with your dookie-covered head. And I likely won't waste my time putting that velvet glove on.

I believe charity and help don't necessarily start at home but rather within. If you want to lose weight and get healthy, no one will make you stop eating all that drive-thru dogshit food but you. If you want to keep eating it, that's up to you, but neither I nor anyone else should have to pay for your stupid choices. The same is true for drinking, drugs, or an addiction to collecting dorky action figures. If you want the world to change, start from within and lead from the front instead of with your blowhorn and soapbox.

I have no desire to tell anyone how he or she has to live. That's up to the person, but again, if you choose stupid, start convincing yourself that boiled wieners taste just like filet mignon, get used to eating no-name macaroni or those 26¢ packages of ramen noodles and forget what real meat, tropical fruit, and Bordeaux taste like, neither I nor anyone else should have to buy them for you because you chose a cause or lifestyle that pays shitty. You made the choice, and if that comes with less-than-desirable lifestyle options, it's yours alone to change; it's not society's responsibility to lick the wounds you created for yourself and enviably the people around you.

I see the world as currently a completely screwed-up place where ideology is in gladiator fight with religion, politics, fantasy, and tradition. That and common sense along with the thick skin of those who went before us have long died at the hands of political correctness. People's personal beliefs and attitudes will always vary, and that's okay. That's what makes us individuals and interesting, but some have the perverse idea that everyone should be equal in every way. That's impossible! The world is made up of people with differing lifestyles, from countless cultures and countries who have different beliefs, and just because they're different from mine or yours or anyone else's doesn't make them wrong or right. And as long as it's not impacting someone else negatively in any real way (not a sad feeling you created from within for whatever "Mommy wipe my nose" reason), then it's all good. It's theirs, and you have no right to stick your schlong in and whiz all over it. However, if you are one of those so-called enlightened people who lean whichever way the trendy wind blows and can't think for yourself, then maybe my drunken ramblings along with a drink or two for yourself while you're reading this will help you unclench your ass cheeks just enough for that eight-foot 2 x 4 to finally fall out.

It should be noted that when I compiled these drunken scribblings into a book-like format, I didn't attempt to keep them in chronological order; instead, I did my best to keep them in order according to the number of shots I had had at the time the thought came to me. On some nights, things got a little blurry as the night went on. Also, at times, it will be somewhat evident what I was doing or what was festering in my mind as I drank. I may have been watching a game on TV, or listening to music, or channel surfing, or screwing around on the internet, or any other number of dumb-shit things—alone, at a party, with friends around, or just hanging with a couple of gassy bulldogs. You will read words and things here that aren't said in church about shit that you won't find in a made-for-TV movie, so be forewarned.

*Disclaimer

Some will take offense at things in this book, but that's probably a good thing because if you're one of those people who take everything out of context and get offended by every little thing in life, I have to ask, what the hell are you doing reading a book called *Grappa Thoughts*? Did you think that anyone's drunken, rambling thoughts were going to be politically correct? If you did, then I suggest you ask your partner to be on the bottom once in a while and start maybe wearing a helmet throughout your daily routine because you can't afford to bump your head any longer as you need to save whatever precious little you have left for everyday things like remembering toilets are for deposits only and chopping wood in the living room is likely frowned upon by your landlord and grounds for eviction.

If you purchased this book and were offended while reading it, maybe you should take a good, long look in the mirror and ask yourself why that was; if you were truly offended by some anonymous drunken insights, you are in fact the bigger problem. If that's the case and you can't stomach another shot physically or in a literary way, may I again suggest that you give it to someone you know who has a sense of humor, someone who sees the lighter side of our screwed-up world, where it has come from, and where it sadly seems to be going, someone with open eyes who sees how we seem hell-bent on castrating each other for trivial garbage like looking at someone with hard eyes. A world where no one is at fault for anything yet everyone is at fault for everything. And all the while as others simply lift a leg and whiz all over everyone and everything for actions from long dead ghosts because of a strange need to quickly point a finger and blame someone else for their shortcomings.

ABBREVIATIONS

$$$$: a moment of true genius; a great money-making idea.

Bulb: a light bulb went off, and I had an ah-ha moment about something that likely wasn't as great as I thought.

TS: true story, usually some stupid shit that actually happened that for whatever reason I suddenly remembered.

Gov't: some luminous, vivid insight about the inner workings of some politician(s) being an asshole and/or the world he or she is making a mess of.

LFBF: looking for Big Foot; a quest for knowledge. Some answer about something.

????: not a clue what the hell I was thinking about when I wrote it.

In-Th: inner thought usually coming after one too many and resembling some form of paranoia.

BM: brilliant mind; Confucius-type shit.

TFUW: today's fucked-up world, how things don't make sense anymore. Or to some, me just showing my age.

Lists: lists are something I was thinking of for one reason or another when I started the night of drinking and was compiled throughout that night or nights and thereby some entries may get more confusing and/or interesting as I went along.

WTF: kind of self-explanatory.

MY SINCERE THANK-YOU

I could never truly thank enough all those who walked far too far along with me and/or at some time joined team Bam and allowed me to be me and accepted and trusted me for who and whatever I am. I will always deep inside feel I owe them far more than I will ever be able to give them even if I live to be 1000. They say that the good die young, so I should be around until at least age 400.

To Mom, Dad, my brother, his family, and our dogs, you have always stood by me despite my many flaws and countless mistakes. I have never thanked you correctly or showed my love very well, but maybe you can allow me to say it here—Thank you, and I love all of you very much.

To my Latin family—The love, respect, caring, and understanding you have all unanimously given me without question or second thoughts have such a special place in my heart. I never really understood why you did this for me, but please know that I'm never letting go of it and hope I'll be able to give back tenfold what you have given me.

To my other family—you know who you are ... Without you guys and the lifetime we have spent together, I'd likely be pumping gas two years out of prison or five-plus years in the grave. You guys mean everything to me. I will always be there for you as you've been there for me.

To the Tigers—You will always hold something for me. Something I have been searching for ever since. Thank you, gentlemen, but no one more than Gif and Duffy. You taught me what real men are.

To the CadominCrew—You have been so great to allow me to be

me and not force my wife to drag me back and apologize for anything stupid I may have or inevitably will do and even on countless occasions joined me in a night or two of whatever, whoever remembers, thank you.

Last but certainly not least, Mi Bella—You brought someone and something out of me that no one before you (including everyone mentioned above and including me) would have ever believed existed in me. You gave me something I never felt I deserved. A part of me, a side that not only feels but also loves unconditionally, and that love burns the brightest and strongest for only you. I plan to spend this lifetime and beyond proving it to you. Te amo, Bella, hoy y siempre.

—Bam

DEDICATION

I dedicate this book to my high school English teacher, Ms. M, who didn't give two squirts about you if you played football or if you couldn't speak in perfect iambic pentameter and to the guidance counselor who dressed somewhere between Cousin Balki and Mr. Rogers from the same school, the man who actually told me my best chance in life was winning on a game show.

Maybe one day we can all sit down, grab a bite to eat, and trade books and war stories with each other ... Oh, wait ... Well, don't worry. I'll still buy you a meal, and you can show me pictures of your annual vacation to the potato farm in Stink Bush, Idaho, tell me all about your cats' hairballs and how your niece was on an episode of *Pimple Popper* and I'll tell you about the company I built with multi millions under management, traveling the world, living in the Caribbean, nights out with famous folks, and how you both silently helped to motivate me to be successful enough to be able to say to you one day (to steal a line from the country singer Toby Keith), "How do you like me now?"

All kidding aside, what you did teach and reinforce in me was something I have taken with me all my life, and that was regardless of what someone else says or thinks about you, it doesn't mean a damn thing if you don't allow it to, and it has no effect on where you go or who you decide to become. Even less when that opinion comes from someone who is going to be nothing more than a distant, vague memory ever after.

I guess memorizing that Shakespearean sonnet and learning how to kiss ass wasn't that important after all, huh?

ONE SHOT

TFUW
The Incredible Hulk in today's world would be given Ritalin and counseling.

In-Th
If you pissed in someone's overpriced cup of Molson Canadian Beer at a hockey game, would he notice because it tasted better?

Bulb
Bowling is the Lada of the sports world.

LFBF
How exactly does Tim Horton's make their coffee taste like they filtered it through a cat?

Gov't
If we go to war to protect our freedoms, why do we elect fucktards to limit them?

Bulb
If you hear, "What do we do for fettuccine alfredo?" coming from a kitchen and someone replies, "Put it in for two minutes," you might not be dining at a future Michelin-starred restaurant.

TS
Once at a bar, I bet some pain-in-the-ass drunk fuck twenty bucks that he couldn't eat the whole blue hockey puck in the urinal thinking he'd barf on himself and leave. It cost me twenty bucks, but he did it without getting sick. It was the best money I ever spent as we watched him walk around the bar for the next half hour or so looking like he blew Papa Smurf. Then he hurled on the beer tub girl.

BM
If time is one of the few things that can't be priced, why isn't it valued more?

Bulb
First hint the world was heading straight into the bowl: it took years before anyone who drank Evian water realized that spelled backward, it's Naive.

LFBF
How is something bought with love? Every fucking place I shop, they take only cash or credit.

TS
Every time my mom made me go with her to the Safeway to get groceries, I'd wait for her to turn her back and toss a Spanish onion into the fresh-made OJ squeezer.

TFUW
Knowledge is power, but unfortunately, the path to success isn't getting a degree in something; rather, it's applying that knowledge. A degree even short of a master's or doctorate more often than not is, however, worth its weight in gold. At four to six grams, that works out to, what? $170? $250?

Bulb
The world is locationally elitist. Christmas lights on a pine tree in a trailer park in July = Trashy people. Christmas lights on a palm tree in South Beach, Miami, in July = Fatty-wacker success.

LFBF
Why are so many countries without any real economy or political system the ones people are most willing to pay top dollar to visit?

BM
Force someone to do something and watch how fast the opposite happens.

TS
My wife says the only song I can dance to is the one that plays only in my head.

LFBF
How the fuck do Amish guys always have clean, ironed, crisp, white shirts?

In-Th
Grappa gives me insight while high school teachers gave me only detention and called my parents. Huh?

TFUW
In days gone by, working for the weekend meant succeeding, but in today's world, working *on* the weekend means survival.

TS
I once blew my nose on the sleeve of some drunk lush who passed out next to me on an overseas plane ride.

Bulb
The only two guys who could rock slippers were Hef and Gigante.

BM
There are two options in life: climbing up or falling down.

Bulb
No one who has ever stayed at a YMCA ever sang the song about it.

TS
For the second time in my life, I hit a snake on a motorbike today—more than 3,000 kilometers and twenty years apart.

LFBF
Are dental plans illegal in Britain?

Bulb
"Mirror, Mirror, on the wall" ... To be the fairest of them all now means you're going to be called either a racist or a sellout by one side or the other.

In-Th
I wonder was it a hate crime when I told the bald prick in the Starbucks line, "Pick a fucking drink, you walking bowling ball!"

TFUW
No one should ever be ashamed or embarrassed by who they are, but they shouldn't expect special treatment because of it either.

Bulb
A one-tooth smile is God's way of telling you, "Stop fucking smiling!"

B.M.
Look behind and see we aren't usually who we think we are.

Bulb
Our male bulldog (the sneaky little shit) has my wife believing he's fucking crippled.

LFBF
Was the inventor of sushi incapable of lighting a fire?

B.M.
Pure aggression without being coupled with clear thought will be anyone's downfall.

TFUW
Def Leppard drummer Rick Allen lost his left arm in a car accident, relearned how to play the drums with one hand, and then went on to sell 25 million copies of their next album. Bieber rhymed baby with baby and then baby ... 'Nuff said.

T.S.
I once damn near killed myself trying to please someone because I mistranslated what he was saying as "It's good enough" because it wasn't good enough for me. I miss you, Duly.

WTF
How the fuck do high school foods teachers earn pensions for teaching kids how to make ants on a log?

Bulb
The silver lining in the coronavirus pandemic is that now I can actually tell window-licking morons and various other dipshits, "Get the fuck away from me!" without nose- picking, snot-eating keyboard warriors calling me out for it.

Bulb
Yawning is the polite way of saying, "Shut the fuck up already. Your opinion is less interesting than purple paint!"

$$$$
Put wine in juice boxes for soccer/hockey moms and junior high teachers.

> Apple—Chardonnay
> Orange—Zinfandel
> Grape—Merlot
> Cranberry—Cabernet Sauvignon
> Peach—Pinot Noir
> Grapefruit—Riesling (they both taste like shit)
> Blueberry—Shiraz
> Mango—Valpolicella

TFUW
I'd put a $10k bet on any famous women from the seventies or eighties including the "Where's the beef?" granny or any of the Golden Girls or even Julie from the *Love Boat* on kicking any of today's modern men's asses.

In-Th
Turi Gardens is my happy spot.

T.S.
The world was doomed when they renewed that dogshit show *Big Brother* for a second season.

In-Th
Kick Noshit in the marbles for liking this reality TV crap and recommending it to me.

Gov't
Boiled down, a politician's only real job is to get reelected.

LFBF
Was Conway Twitty's hair actually waterproof, or was it just chia seeds on a hockey helmet he had cut and colored so no one would know the truth?

T.S.
Worst question ever: What song were you conceived to?

LFBF
Christian rock? If you're going to be a rock god, what the hell is the point without all the debauchery, stupidity, and crazy shit?

TFUW
My tech-challenged beautiful wife just tried to teach my tech-impaired mom how to use Whatsapp, which my mom kept calling "What's it?" It was a slow-motion car accident that I couldn't look away from. It was also the most painful thirty minutes (that seemed like three hours) I'd been through in a while.

B.M.
Simple thought—Live the life you choose however you see fit. Do whatever floats your boat and makes you happy, and I promise I will never try to impose my views or ideals on you. Just don't expect me or anyone else to pay for it. In return, show me the same respect. Do this, and as long as your world doesn't physically or financially hurt mine or my family's, you and I will never have a problem, but try once to change my world, reach over my fence, or steal from my cookie jar and it'll be on, bitch!

In-Th

I saw a K-car earlier today. I thought they went the same way as the Pinto had and all dissolved in the rain by now. Huh?

LFBF

In what universe is a drive-thru consistently slower than walking in and ordering?

Bulb

Suburban driving can be defined as don't pay attention, drive to the rhythm of the crappy trendy tune you're blaring and singing along to, and then blame everyone else for being in your way.

B.M.

Hunger teaches, desperation forces, confusion and complacency allows.

Bulb

Everyone now being masked up has made mumblers almost completely useless.

Bulb

TV steals time, money, brain cells, common sense, cognitive reasoning, fear, reasons to try, mental acuity, understanding, thinking ability, reading skills, desire, life …

TFUW

Fees, interest, and taxes are all the same—something stolen from my pocket to be put in the pocket of someone who didn't earn it.

Bulb

The way someone parks is a great indication of how selfish and self-absorbed that person is.

WTF
Disney is so creative ... FYI, caterpillars becoming butterflies were the original Cinderella.

Bulb
"The sun will come up tomorrow" unless you're in Seattle. Been there, like, three times, never saw the damn thing once.

B.M.
All wallets and purses empty faster than they fill.

T.S.
I've made almost 12,000% off a handful of pennies that were there for the taking by anyone paying attention.

LFBF
How many times since the millennial start have the Martians said, "We don't have to invade. Mankind has less than fifty years to go before it totally implodes. We can do that standing on our slimy green heads."

Bulb
Money can't buy happiness maybe, but what it does buy is options, and a lack of options buys only resentment.

TFUW
Some jerk-off hair shampoo company ran an ad saying that it was vegan. No shit? Never once had I thought shampoo was made with leftover T-bones and bouillon cubes.

T.S.
Technology and I are *not* friends.

Bulb

I love church billboards that read "God Forgives." He kind of has to, doesn't he? After all, isn't he the one who supposedly created all of us?

WTF

Jessica Simpson wrote a memoir she called *Open Book*. I think she titled it that so her fans would know what to do with it and not confuse the both of them like books obviously did her. I have to assume her follow-up book will be a comic or a coloring book.

Bulb

There is far more to every story.

$$$$

Teach time-management to doctors.

T.S.

I have severe allergies to bullshit and stupidity and have very harsh reactions to either when directly exposed to them.

LFBF

If you're that dumb fuck who gives a full car length at a drive-thru, why? Park, put your helmet on, and go inside.

Bulb

You'll never reach your promised land if you never leave your beach.

TFUW

Being five and dimed now works out to a $50 and a C note.

B.M.

The smell of victory always stinks to the ones who lost.

Gov't
Naturalization is the government's way of saying, "We're not going to be picking the weeds or mowing the grass any longer, but make sure your taxes are paid on time, and P.S.: Your taxes are going up because we've just created naturalized spaces throughout the city."

TFUW
A social influencer is someone whose opinion means less to me than that of an airline's employee of the year. I actually had to look it up to make sure I knew what they were—pathetic wannabes with too many participation ribbons and mommy's and daddy's credit cards.

Bulb
If you went to university just to get a diploma, you didn't learn anything.

LFBF
When did there become a middle ground between right and wrong?

B.M.
Anyone who acts on his or her insecurities will eventually be defined by them.

Bulb
Everyone has a gift or talent for something; unfortunately, most never make use of theirs and end up relying on other abilities they are not as good at.

WTF
Free housing for the homeless? You're truly creating the cut that never heals. Stupid fucking government dickwipes.

LFBF
Why do Martians visit only the stupid, cousin-breeder folks?

TFUW
The more I watch the news, the more I want to be a pirate on the high seas.

Bulb
Seinfeld was right—Cops and garbage men do basically the same job.

Bulb
The greatest things in life make you sweat, leave you breathless, and make your heart beat through your chest.

LFBF
Who the fuck told Ben Stiller he could act? Whoever it was must have been a hell of an actor.

T.S.
The best naps I've ever taken were when my wife got the box set of *Little House on The Prairie*.

Gov't
If a bike lane is within a rock's throw and a putz is riding his bike still down the middle of the real road instead in the bike lane created especially for him, maybe he should be fined the first time, and if he still don't get the idea, then he should be turned into a speed bump.

LFBF
While I applaud Thomas Crapper and his many inventions and advancements in bathroom stuff (Yeah, look it up—That was his real name), how the fuck did anyone come up with the brilliant idea of making the chair filled with running water that you sit on with all your weight and forcefully push chocolate nuggets out of your naked ass and think, *We should make these things out of porcelain glass*?

Bulb
My fur alarm is more regular than a German train schedule.

WTF
Halloween night, and the scariest thing on TV is an old episode of the *Lawrence Welk Show*. What the hell happened to us?

B.M.
Maybe if we ditched those "Do not attempt this at home" disclaimers, we could truly start making the world a better place.

TFUW
Sirens are warning signs of a crappy neighborhoods and/or lifestyles.

LFBF
I wonder if my nimrod neighbor who flicks his cigarette butts at my trash cans realizes they're actually his.

Bulb
Gift bags have replaced fruitcakes as the most recycled Christmas items.

B.M.
Winning is two-thirds just knowing how the game is played.

Gov't
If zombies can't do snow and cold, you'd think we'd be pretty safe here in Canada, but for some reason, we elect them.

LFBF
Why do we torture dogs to learn to shake a paw and roll over and do other meaningless tricks but give cats a pass?

Bulb
IKEA makes Tinker Toys for adults.

T.S.
I've made presentations in front of countless numbers of people from multimillionaires to convicted killers literally.

TFUW
If I slip and fall on the ice, can I now sue Mother Nature?

Gov't
Countless small businesses and various others privately employed were forced to take enormous financial haircuts for the greater good during the coronavirus, but not one politician lost a single penny. Huh?

B.M.
Hiding from responsibility only makes finding your way back harder.

LFBF
Hoarders on social assistance? How the fuck does that work? I'm thinking the system might need some major retuning.

Bulb
The glass is always half-full for someone who's thirsty enough.

TFUW
Kids need to look beyond the bank of mom and dad before they should expect to be treated as adults ... Unless they're in their forties, 'cause by then, it's too late and the respect ship has both sailed and sunk.

LFBF
Was Coca-Cola healthier when they put cocaine in it? Because it's basically a flavored version of crack to sweatpants-wearing, Skip the Dishes, video game playing, basement dwellers now.

Bulb
Jeans tucked into cowboy boots on dudes means they should be wearing tennis shoes.

B.M.
Reality is an economic perception.

LFBF
Why do we have First World countries and Third World countries but no Second, Fourth, or Fifth World countries? Was the guy who came up with that ideology the victim of a piss-poor, First World public school math curriculum and unable to count?

WTF
I was on the phone parked outside a bank and watched a little old man take off his toque and hand it to a homeless guy sleeping in front, and as he got up to take it, the homeless guy dropped his cell phone ... FTW.

T.S.
I have all the flexibility of a 2 x 4.

LFBF
Men might think they wear the pants, but women know they have the ability to get men to take them off, so who really calls the shots?

Bulb
Going to the dentist as a kid, going to see a lawyer as an adult, going to the vet with a dog, or seeing strippers as an underage youth all sparked the same uneasy feeling of impending doom.

B.M.
Pay for skills and knowledge, not an ego or a diploma.

TFUW
The coronavirus has shown us all some major holes in our health care and financial systems, schools, government, food chains, border security, and beyond. Nothing will be changed or fixed. (Written April 5, 2020.)

LFBF
Why is shit that gets stuck in our teeth the go-to food at movie theaters?

Bulb
The secret to life, business, and childbirth are the same—You need to push.

B.M.
Using a cheap lawyer, accountant, or dentist will eventually cost you a fortune.

Gov't
Governments are great at feeding Kiyosaki's rats just enough for them to think they're getting ahead.

Bulb
The most inspirational seat in the house has a button on the back to flush with.

T.S.
I hate peacocks—the noisy, fat birds and pretentious people.

Bulb
Life was never meant to be lived on Facebook or in a Starbucks lineup.

LFBF
How much stock do you put in a lazy guy with cheesy dust and taco bits on his shirt who tells you that he's super busy?

In-Th

If you're dealing with either a Britney or a Taylor, you have an 85 percent chance of having to finish it yourself, and the other 15 percent run a fifty-fifty chance of being disappointed.

B.M.

Sooner or later, we all turn around and read the writing on the wall. Then we either climb or fall.

TFUW

Political correctness in the 1980s ... Michael Jordan, Wayne Gretzky, Barry Bonds, etc., *we need you guys to sit out a couple games so we can give Walter Chiznuk some game time. After all, his mom paid for all the participation trophies at the end of the season, and she does bring orange slices for everyone every game.*

Gov't

So we can't show criminals pictures on TV or report the names of young offenders regardless of what horrible shit they did, and federal inmates are set to be vaccinated before the people who lost their livelihoods and life savings due to the virus for the greater good? Who is actually being protected?

Bulb

A life without scars is a life that was never actually lived.

B.M.

The guy standing beside you isn't your competition. The one in the mirror is.

TFUW

Stopped at a bakery/cafe place to grab an espresso earlier today, and this is what the little girl I'll call Britney who was in line behind me said: *"I'd like a milk chocolate ganache cupcake please. Do they come in diary free?"* Damn. Today's world is a pampered mess.

TWO SHOTS

Bulb
One-ply toilet paper is like telling your clients or customers that you don't really value them.

T.S.
I once took a huge Taco Bell–infused coiler on the bathroom floor at the place I worked knowing my dumb-fuck prick boss would likely step in it. He did.

B.M.
Dream big, and then double it.

TFUW
People once rubbed bald guys' heads for good luck. Is that now a hate crime or some fucked-up form of sexual assault?

Gov't
I'm politically agnostic.

Bulb
Prisons are full of volunteers acting like victims while airplanes are full of hostages who voluntarily paid.

B.M.

Tomorrow's wisdom rarely comes from much more than today's disappointment.

LFBF

Why the hell is Jack short for John?

Bulb

I think my female bulldog has a gummy bear addiction.

T.S.

In junior high, I used to draw wangs and balls in teacher workbooks just to see if they actually taught from them. It was a bitch trying to keep a straight face knowing when and or if the odd one found them.

Bulb

Nothing will help you until you help yourself and stop looking for someone to do it for you.

LFBF

Do fools trying to fool and/or outsmart everyone ever fool anyone other than the fools in their mirror?

T.S.

Globalization is Star Trek thinking.

In-Th

I think that cranky fuck ex-neighbor barbecued a cat or a bag of his wife's old wigs in his garage before he sold his place a few weeks ago. You still get a whiff of some nasty, smelly shit when the wind blows past it.

B.M.

Life is nothing more than a game of paying attention and being adaptable.

LFBF

If you eat McD's and Taco Bell–type shit every day, does that mean you've already given up?

Bulb

If Domino's can say what they make is pizza, I should be allowed to buy a Toyota Corolla and sell it as a Porsche.

Bulb

Ballwasher—199_ something. My apologies—2021.

Gov't

Our fearless leader wants to ban specific guns solely because they look scary. We voted this fool in twice.

WTF

If this bulldog of mine farts one more time lying beside me on the couch, I'm either corking his ass with my wife's scented candle or making him sleep in the garage.

LFBF

What the fuck is a vegetarian cheeseburger?

T.S.

I used to rub chili peppers on the computer keyboard and phone of this prick I worked with who owed me money and made every excuse not to pay me back, so everyone thought he was typhoid Mary by noon every day.

TFUW

A woman who works for my wife has a husband whom everyone calls Leprechaun because he's short and from Ireland. What the hell do I do not to commit PC suicide?

Bulb
Stupidity is the best toy ever.

B.M.
The hardest place to find safe refuge in is anywhere where someone else has fucked up royally before you.

LFBF
If Kermit fucked a head of lettuce, would their lovechild be a French salad?

Bulb
Evolution is fucked. Horses eat grass, shit on everything, and are peaceful. Man eats everything, smokes grass, shits in the ocean he eats from, and has no idea what peace is. Marvin the Martian wears grass on his head, doesn't have a mouth to eat with, never shits, and is consumed with blowing the world up.

T.S.
In high school, a math class a teacher had a nervous breakdown; instead of calling for help, we all just snuck out.

LFBF
Why are all ghosts bald?

Bulb
I remember some folklore about that the original Santa Claus story came from Germany in like the 1600s thus making him the first dictator of forced labor camps that likely used children long before the Nazis.

WTF
What the hell are assless chaps? Aren't chaps with asses called pants?

B.M.
If you choose to stay in a room full of dullards because they make you feel like a rock star genius, you are in fact the dumbest one there.

T.S.
I once convinced the dim-witted, know-it-all brother of a guy who lets us hunt on his land that Indians got their sources of vitamin C back in the day by eating the undigested contents of animals' stomachs. The putz tossed back a handful of the smelly, fuzzy shit before puking all over the place for the next hour or so. I guess he didn't know everything after all.

TFUW
Millennials order shit off the internet one item at a time and have it shipped directly to their parents' basement with six layers of plastic wrap and half a pound of packing peanuts and pay for it via online banks that have building-sized computers housed with enormous A/C units, but straws are what's fucking up the world and need to be banned. Huh?

LFBF
Why do so many women want bad boys but still want to change them?

Bulb
Your life sucks if you find yourself waiting out the washing machine as it cycles.

LFBF
Do high heels and long-neck beer bottles make short guys feel inferior?

T.S.
When I was in university, I worked at a grocery store where I'd cut labels off the cans of cat food and wrote "Tuna—25¢" on the top of them and then toss them into the employee discount bin in the back

knowing that a pain-in-the-ass, thirty-something cashier would buy them for the poor, dumb bastard who had married her.

TFUW
"How soon they forget" has been replaced by "They never really understood but bitch about it anyway."

B.M.
Every young man and woman goes to war. Some on foreign soil, some with the other people or places around them, and some without even leaving the couch.

Bulb
Telling me I need to wear a pink shirt on national bullying day is actually bullying.

T.S.
When my male bulldog wakes suddenly from a bad dream, I feel I have failed him somehow, but then, I think all he does is eat, sleep, and shit, so how bad could it really be?

WTF
Why are they called G strings if they're in the shape of a *T*?

Bulb
Rice flour tortillas are about as useful as wet toilet paper.

B.M.
Marrying for money is the hardest way to make money.

LFBF
Why are all the cool cowboy songs sung by skinny, little, balding fucks who look like they're trying to shoplift a potato down the front of their extra-small Levis?

Bulb
Staffers who don't disappoint are potentially future competition.

TFUW
Without technology, you could rob a bank by simply asking a math question.

T.S.
I do a great deal of the cooking in our house not because I'm a gourmet; I'm more of the Swedish Muppet chef, a self-delusional glutton with a midlife spread. I like cooking big family meals because for an extra couple of hours of work, I end up with a fair amount of free time for the next two-three days because of all the leftovers.

Bulb
The British weather nerd on the TV looks like a by-product of Trump Jr. and a constipated giraffe.

LFBF
Is playing the banjo a secret cry for help?

TFUW
In today's fucked-up world, Mr. Myagi would be charged by workers' comp for picking on Daniel-son.

Bulb
A forty-eight-hour hangover still beats a two-hour Disney movie.

LFBF
Is life trying to tell you something when you realize your chosen career has you driving a twenty-year-old rusty Dodge Neon and the lead singer of Metallica has a Ferrari worth $1.4 million?

TFUW
Did Clint Eastwood cry when John Wayne died knowing he was one of the only ones left?

LFBF
Why the fuck did that little midget in the tower on *Fantasy Island* always cream into his doll-sized chinos when he saw "zee plane"? It was not like he was ever banging one of the guests who got off of it in any episode I ever saw. Look it up. He called himself a midget before you right fighters have heads that explode over a word.

In-Th
Not sure why Fishbelly's and Marilyn's yard smells like onions and cabbage.

T.S.
When I need to get going, I often use work as an excuse and say that my boss is a dick. It's true. He is. (I own the company).

B.M.
The rich get richer during times of disease and strife because while the masses hold pity parties and see who can bitch and cry the loudest in hopes of being rescued or bailed out, the rich see any change from the everyday norm as an opportunity, not an excuse.

TFUW
Just saw an ad on TV for a fifties-and-over dating website that had a disclaimer that said, "For those eighteen and older …" Fuck me. Today's childproof, bubble-wrapped world.

LFBF
Is it just me, or does anyone else find it to be interesting and ironic that in 2019, Canada legalized marijuana and a few months later,

some shithead ate a herpes-riddled bat causing the world to change and was followed by Canadians losing their minds out of paranoia and all but fighting in the streets over ass wipes?

Bulb
Two witless, moronic twenty-somethings just came to the door trying to get me to donate to the rain forest or pink unicorns or underweight cows or something. I want a waterproof sign that reads, "If you want money for your dipshit cause, or if you are some politico shithead trying to empty my pockets, or have fourteen-year-old warehoused cookies and nuts for sale, or think we should shave our heads and hail your quasi-god Ali Shibi, get the fuck off my property."

Bulb
All these goofball new subscription channels that advertise on cable channels with some must-see program led by some superstar has-been are becoming a pain in the ass. I figure TV has four, maybe five years left before it completely implodes.

B.M.
Whatever scares you the most has a better than average chance of earning you a very handsome profit because you'll likely pay so much more attention to it.

LFBF
Does Starbucks crank up the shitty music they pipe in as a way to cover the fact that three out of five kids working behind the counters don't listen to what anyone says to them?

T.S.
The best insult I ever got was, "You'd make a great politician," but it was from some PC dillweed, so who the fuck was ever going to take him seriously?

WTF

Residents of a tent city homeless encampment were told they had twenty-four hours to vacate via an email from civil enforcement, and in response, they tried to plan a protest via social media. Seriously? Email? Social Media? They're fucking homeless!

TFUW

I can only imagine how disappointed opportunity is knocking on a door, jingling the change in his pocket, and waiting for the guy who's looking at him via his doorbell cam to open the door but knowing he likely won't because he doesn't recognize him or want to pause his video game.

LFBF

Dog the Bounty Hunter—who the fuck were you kidding? I saw a cameraman outrun your daughter while the rest of you were coughing up Marlboro dust. I guess that's why you go after crackheads and bike thieves, huh?

Bulb

A dream that goes unpursued isn't a dream; it's a fantasy.

B.M.

If you ram things down people's throats, you will inevitably end up with pushback and vomit on your shoes.

Bulb

Here's a handy tip for all the shitty drivers: Those pretty little lines painted on the roads are there for you to stay between, *not* to try to drive over and keep under your vehicle. You're driving a car, not landing a jumbo jet.

LFBF

Why is it a matter of eating crow after someone has proven you to be shoveling shit?

B.M.
The unknown is the only place you'll find results you don't already have.

Bulb
Words can hurt only when we allow them to because words are just words. Causing others physical harm because of the color of their skin or their accent is racism. If the worst thing that happens to you today is that someone called you a name regardless of what it was, you still have a pretty damn good day going. Try to keep perspective. How many people around the world who don't have food, clean water, or shelter would gladly trade places with you in return for just being called a word by some inbred, ignorant asshole?

TFUW
Parents who allow their kids to act the way they do in their backyards when they're out in public are the ones who actually need spankings.

In-Th
Don't ask the kid at the coffee shop with the blue hair if his pen exploded until after he hands you your coffee.

LFBF
I have a five-hundred-pound statue of Buddha in my backyard behind a pond with a giant torii gate/waterfall, and I just picked up a Halloween light called "fires of hell" to reflect off it. Is that sacrilegious?

Gov't
Why do I and everyone else have to do our personal shit on our own time when in an election year, our political leaders for what—eight, nine months?—do nothing but campaign to keep their chair-moistening, slack-ass faux jobs?

B.M.
Two bulls (or bullheads) dropping plunkets in the same pasture will never end well.

Bulb
I realize some people look up at clouds daydreaming and see all kinds of kooky shit. I look up at them and see rain, go back inside, and get back to fucking work.

LFBF
If fruit such as pineapple doesn't belong on pizza, then someone please explain to me why tomato sauce—not dorky, new age, goofball sauces such as barbecue, alfredo, and that super-gross coconut goop—which comes from a fruit is okay (though coconut is a fruit too).

B.M.
Your life's high-water mark should always be in the future.

Bulb
The most powerful drug in the world is adrenaline, and anyone who has ever truly tasted its sweet nectar is likely addicted for life.

LFBF
There's more than one way to skin a cat? What the hell does anyone do with skinned cats?

Bulb
If you fight for it, make sure it's something you actually want in case you win.

In-Th
The window doesn't last.

Bulb

Leaders either get past their fears and stage fright or get replaced and forgotten.

B.M.

Higher education is a sign of money, not intelligence.

TFUW

"Plant and soil diversity" is the millennial way of saying, "growing weeds."

LFBF

Was the term *cock-tail* party seventies code for orgy?

T.S.

In second grade, I took a whiz into the teacher's wastepaper basket and covered it with some kid's crappy artwork because she wouldn't let me go outside for recess but left the classroom herself so she could go have a smoke in the teachers' lounge all because I had pointed out that I'd seen her smoking during our lesson about not smoking in health class earlier that day.

Bulb

I learned early on to never meet my heroes of youth; more often than not, I usually needed to pick better ones. Dave, you were the exception to that.

B.M.

Fortune cookies are nuggets of wisdom only to fools and the foolish.

Bulb

Home may be where the heart is, but work is where the paycheck and a sense of accomplishment come from.

TFUW
"Fake it until you make it" is likely the battle cry of countless bullet eaters who took shitty advice from others who never made it but saw themselves as gurus of knowledge despite having very little if any.

B.M.
Insights come when you allow yourself to see things without judgment.

LFBF
Were mic stands invented for serial, fucked-up singers to lean on?

T.S.
I love to skydive but absolutely hate flying … Huh?

Bulb
The world will always be burning and storms will always be turning except for those who can weather them and manage to find their way beyond them. They'll find success welcoming them on the other side. For those who can't and don't, success will sadly often be accused of nothing more than inciting envy.

TFUW
One of the funniest things I heard in 2020: "The government needs to do a lockdown of restaurants, bars, and gyms for at least a couple of weeks and get this thing under control so we don't overwhelm our health care system." It was coming from a guy sitting at a table in a coffee shop.

LFBF
Why do gas pumps and drive-up cash machines have braille on them?

$$$$
If you want to get rich, forget about building a better mousetrap; just find something that mankind will become dependent on or allow them to become lazier.

Bulb
I do any and all writing with pen and paper first. That way, my creativity is never limited to a battery's lifespan.

B.M.
The goal line is always the farthest away for those who never start.

LFBF
How many people go on *Ancestry.com* to find out about their rich family history and end up saying, "Ohhhhh ... So we have webbed toes because great-great-grandma and great-great-grandpa were first cousins."

T.S.
If you want to live outside societal norms, you have only two options: get far beyond them and live life on your own terms, or get run over by them and live in constant fear of them.

Bulb
Garbage Can Brian puts out so many Christmas lights and decorative crap at Christmas time that lost pilots and concert goers often end up way off course passing through or above our neighborhood. I expect to see three guys on donkeys riding up any day now.

Gov't
Streets named after politicians should be only in shitty neighborhoods but never are.

Bulb

There's nothing scarier than the unknown. There's also nothing more rewarding than venturing into the unknown.

LFBF

In what fucking world would Santa be a jolly guy? He flies around in the dead of winter in a convertible pulled by a bunch of gassy, smelly animals that he hasn't eaten yet, crawls his fat ass through filthy fireplaces, and eats countless shitty homemade cookies (adding to his fat gut and diabetes) only to go home to his place in the permanently wintery north to his naggy wife who constantly complains about his staying out all night and keeps them both dressed in matching red velvet and velour only to pick which whiny, forced, kid laborers he'll feed to his inbreed reindeer until the Mrs, finally lets him out again next December 24.

Bulb

No great memory was ever made by farting into couch cushions.

B.M.

Bullets come in many, many forms.

LFBF

Do outie belly buttons still exist, or have they been done away with because of political correctness?

B.M.

Big risk equals big reward if you do big preparation and groundwork first. Otherwise, it's just big luck.

TFUW

Because I think it's an idiot day (you don't need a special day to let the people you care about know it), I thought I'd give some inside info about how fools looking to get laid actually get screwed on Valentine's Day instead. Hershey's Kisses are just twenty-some chocolate chips individually wrapped that you just paid $14.99 for in a 35¢ red box.

T.S.
If someone really wanted to steal from me, all he or she would have to do is ask me to buy something off the internet and just watch as I did everything wrong.

B.M.
Choices and decisions separate winners and chronic losers.

LFBF
If you rubbed wrinkle cream on your junk, would that give you a boner, and would you get the same result if you didn't *rub* it in?

Bulb
Hurt feelings are like the common cold. Everyone has had them, no one wants them, and they're usually a lot less severe than people say they are.

B.M.
Driving hard to the hoop can happen only if you actually show up to play and not just collect a participation ribbon.

LFBF
Why the fuck is YouTube running French ads for me between songs? The only French I know are French fries, French toast and Paris, France.

Bulb
If you subscribe to one of those food delivery services that bring you a box full of uncooked food and spices and a step-by-step recipe card, you don't cook dinner; you assemble it. You're in fact somewhere

between a puzzle maker and the guy ordering dinner in the drive-thru via a clown's head. Go buy your own green pepper and learn how to cook it.

T.S.
My beautiful wife had a birthday party for me a couple of years ago and invited our CadominCrew over for it, but she warned me beforehand not to get out of control with the guys as sometimes we get a little stupid and nutty.

The men went to the den to shoot the shit and just hang out as the women stuck around the kitchen for about an hour. After they downed all the tequila we had brought back from Mexico a few weeks earlier, Karen, Rich's wife, found my limoncello and peach grappa, and the ladies downed that also before we came back to join them still sober.

Within an hour, we had to call an ambulance for eighty-five-year-old Agnes (not her real name). She was fine, just shockingly pissed—by her own doing. She spent the night at our place and fell out of bed twice. Yeah, the men are the bad ones …

TFUW
I stopped by a Canadian department store that had gotten its start specializing in tires and car parts; I was waiting in line for a battery. The guy in front of me was there to get winter tires put on his car and was talking with the nineteen-year-old clerk I'll call Taylor (for semi-obvious reasons).

> Customer: I need a set of winter tires put on my car please.
> Taylor: Sure. What kind of car is it?
> Customer: It's a Tesla.
> Taylor: Oh, I love those! They're my favorite! How do you spell it?

THREE SHOTS

LFBF
How the fuck do you win a trophy for showing up and losing?

T.S.
Duly, you are the toughest tough guy with the kindest heart I have ever known. Sleep good, Valhalla.

$$$$
New slogan for Air Canada: "We're Not Happy Until You're Not Happy." Truth in advertising.

T.S.
My uncle Jackie's pallbearers actually went by the names Torch, Skinhead, Joyce, Winston, Fingers, Jeffers, Moses, McConkey, Smiley, Bamford, Creek, Gene, and Mr. Brown, and the priest, their dear friend, went by Reverend Elvis.

Bulb
I'm going to ask the next dickhead thinking he's playing Mario Kart driving like a prick if his baby is a Pontiac or a Geo Metro just to watch his head pop off.

LFBF
If green represents jealousy and red represents anger, what moron came up with the Christmas color scheme?

Gov't
Email is the most passive, chickenshit, unproductive way of pretending to be in business today but a staple for a government job. Huh?

B.M.
If you have a special theater or restaurant you love, never look backstage or go in the kitchen.

WTF
The world seems to have an overactive gland producing too much fucktardism as of late.

Bulb
Jeopardy's teachers' tournaments are about as hard as boiled spaghetti in seniors' homes. (I kept that classy and could have said something else that's likely super soft in senior homes).

In-Th
If this book sells more than seventeen copies, I'll apply as a writer for crappy made-for-TV movies on the Hallmark channel.

T.S.
Once when we were traveling around Lake Titicaca, my buddy an I (both with varying cases of Montezuma's revenge) went to a restaurant/disco. While waiting in line, I went to use the bathroom only to discover that the toilet wasn't much more than a hole in the floor you squatted over with no toilet paper, but I did my thing, took the curtain off the wall, wiped my backside with it, and carefully hung it back up.

Then it was my buddy's turn ... Before I could tell him anything, he made a beeline to the toiletless bathroom. Three minutes later, the whole place heard a loud *"Fuuuuuuck!"* Ten minutes later, he walked out with no socks and missing half his shirt.

TFUW
Do we even test for drivers' licenses any longer, or do we just hand them out like they do with grades in school nowadays?

Bulb
Like most things in life, you find them when you stop focusing only on them.

LFBF
Why do people use pens, key chains, and even bus benches to advertise on? Who the fuck reads any of those things?

TFUW
If today's world is now the opposite of the overly self-indulgent, extravagant 1980s, why does anyone old enough to remember them still secretly live in the music, television, and movies from that time and Hollywood remakes all of it?

T.S.
The biggest animal I've ever seen outside a circus or a zoo was a twenty-foot anaconda.

Bulb
Most ten-gallon hats are full of nine and a half gallons of nothing.

Bulb
If Justin Bieber and Justin Trudeau had a charity boxing match, I'd likely read the ingredients on a package of baloney rather than watch it because regardless of who won, the fake meat ingredients would be more interesting than either of them.

B.M.
The phrases *Piss on it* and *Just sign on the dotted line* should never be done with the same instrument.

WTF
The damn bulldog just farted on the remote.

Gov't
The world is going to turn this coronavirus thing into paranoia and fuck everything up, and governments everywhere will find ways to fill their pockets from it. (Written February 29, 2020.)

T.S.
If anything's ever going to get done to your satisfaction, it will always fall on the same person.

TFUW
Having your cake and eating it too now means that someone else is at fault for something.

Bulb
The only cup the Montreal Canadiens will ever touch again is the one in their jocks.

WTF
Why the fuck do I work and pay taxes so others don't have to?

T.S.
Years ago, we got blind drunk with the old dudes from Nazareth after a show, and one of them tipped my buddy Kenny $100 for babysitting him.

Bulb
Old folks' homes of the future will look like Jackson Pollock paintings with odd floatation devices because of all the wrinkly tattoos

that no one will be able to tell what they once were and the large number of women with built-in, overinflated, saggy tray tables with nipples at waist height.

LFBF
Does the coffee shop industry get secret kickbacks from somewhere for hiring so many fucktards with green hair who don't listen?

B.M.
Even the clock will fuck with you if you let it.

Bulb
It's so refreshing to deal with real professionals instead of internet self-trained mutts who think they are.

In-Th
Is there a secret global agenda to cover the world in Nerf noodles?

Bulb
The only ones who go to their graves without regrets are those who never attempted anything beyond what they already knew.

Bulb
Producing milk from cows brings the farmer good fortune but costs him a fortune when his unwed daughter produces it.

T.S.
I once was so fucked up in a Latin American karaoke bar that I couldn't find the bathroom and pissed in a potted plant just steps away from the guy with the microphone.

Bulb
YouTube ads are full of nerd shit.

Gov't
Those who know lots of shit don't often give a shit, and those who give a shit often don't know shit.

LFBF
Do horse-riding cowboys get carsick?

Bulb
I think my parents' one neighbor is whom the TV show *Sanford and Son* was based on.

TFUW
To all the parents who try to retrofit the error of their ways via their kids and bubble wrap them to the size of the Michelin Man, two words: *Todd Marinovich*. Look him up. You'll understand.

T.S.
I once ate an okra salad, and for a week, my shit smelled like something had died in me.

LFBF
Do guys who make horror movies know something we don't?

WTF
Those fucking hillbillies who run around the Florida Everglades barefoot hunting for python snakes: What the fuck is wrong with you? Couldn't you find a better job like field testing ballistic tank tops or shark fishing by dangling a pork chop from your junk? Push comes to shove and truth be told, I'd still vote for any of you over any of the weirdoes and wack-jobs our countries have because you guys aren't afraid to get your hands dirty.

LFBF

Why do onions and garlic keep vampires at bay and somehow apples do the same for doctors?

Bulb

Dentists are the best-paid sadists.

B.M.

Hurt comes only to those who can feel.

LFBF

Why do so many mass shootings happen at places of enlightenment and/or higher learning?

T.S.

In high school, I used to color in the numbers on the locker lock of a kid who was chronically late with a black felt just to enjoy the show. He and I are members of the same gun club now.

TFUW

We, the masses, spend our first twenty or twenty-five years learning *what to think* and half-truths and then the next forty years or so climbing continuous financial mountains and focusing on trivial distractions like Kim K's fat ass or meatless burgers while looking and fantasizing about finding some untouchable Shangri-La upon retirement on pay that allows little more than survival only to be butt-raped upon our death one last time by being taxed beyond the grave and continuing the same cycle for every generation ever after.

The rich and elite avoid all this by attending private schools that teach them *how to think* rather than what to think and spend their working years refining their knowledge to pass it and their wealth on to the next generation. This is why the rich get richer and the poor drink Timmy's, drive cake donut, mass-marketed crap, yell at the TV, and vote for reality TV shit.

B.M.

The reality of humankind is that you have to allow each person to figure it out for himself or herself and hope the majority have the capacity to do it.

In-Th

I hope it rains enough tonight to wash my piss off the deck.

Bulb

I have been both halves. The other half lives just fine.

Bulb

Driving anything yellow means you could be talked into anything.

T.S.

My wife (from South America) and I lived in Costa Rica for several years, and once, when she went home alone to visit family, she took some of my old photos along to show some of her friends who hadn't met me. One was a photo of me and a couple of buds hanging at some club with Ron Jeremy. (She didn't know who he was.) She had a hell of a lot of questions for me when she got back.

LFBF

When did Hollywood stop trying and start saying, "Just hire Joey's special kid"?

Bulb

Using an MLM to look after your finances is the equivalent of getting a mail-order trophy wife from a boys' reformatory.

T.S.

I have mad respect for people who solve rather than create problems.

LFBF
Is a pearl just dried jism from a clam that formed a ball because of the constant ocean currents washing over it?

B.M.
So many things in life cost a shitload of money, but effort is not one of them.

TFUW
I don't give you the finger or swear at you based on the color of your skin or because you're male or female or whatever. I do it because you're a shitty driver, and if you're going to be on the road, you should be either taking the bus or be a speed bump.

T.S.
The only time my inner voice takes a break and stops nattering enough for my creativity to truly take over is after number four.

Bulb
The fucking exec who came up with or okayed the brilliant idea of ice cubes in a ball shape to take GE to the refrigerator promised land likely got his cubes handed to him when they fired him.

B.M.
Live your life, not other people's.

$$$$
Some may think I'm a dinosaur (Adina), but my first annual Guns and Grappa event brought in over $400k within a month, and I've had a waiting list ever since.

LFBF
What's worse, dumb-fuck kids eating Tide pods or supporting them ever after?

Bulb

Dr. Dave, the onset of the coronavirus fucked you harder than anyone else I know.

Bulb

The media has developed a very efficient way to instill fear in the
underinformed.

WTF

I can't be the only one who thinks that the only difference between
Cheetos and Kraft mac and cheese is the amount of water used to
make them and the length of time they sit on the shelves.

T.S.

I made more than my last boss did by the time I was twenty-seven.

TFUW

Everyone is free not to follow society's rules, but they should still be
made to face the results if they don't.

Bulb

If someone mistakes you for a used-car salesmen, you are *not* dressed
for success tie or no tie.

B.M.

Three options in life:

    A) Get on the bus.
    B) Drive the bus.
    C) Get run over by the bus.

Bulb

I went grocery shopping earlier today, and the place had one of
those live fish counters with lobsters, crabs, and other shellfish. It

was decorated with buoys and fishnets and plastic lobsters and fish hanging all over the walls, which got me thinking that if the lobsters in the tank had feelings, they must have felt like lost tourists who had stumbled into a headhunter village.

Bulb
No one on his or her deathbed ever said, "Maybe I should have aimed lower."

T.S.
I have an old pickup I call Rusty for semi-obvious reasons, an anniversary bike I call Moe, and a fully tricked out, full-size Range Rover I call Matilda because it sounded semi exotic, fun, and pricy as hell to maintain.

LFBF
If a cat dumps in its walk-in litter box and afterward licks its paws and its turd-cutting third eye clean, why would anyone want to cuddle with it? At least a dog shits and then wipes its ass on the grass or carpet, not with its tongue.

Bulb
Described video has to be one of the dumbest inventions of all time right up there with diet water and the no-phone ... Some clueless bastard describing a show poorly in a monotone ... I guarantee that if I ever went blind, I wouldn't be *watching* TV to listen to it. P.S.: Shaw Cable, stop changing me for this shit.

T.S.
I try to treat everyone equally unless they're lazy and/or stupid; then, I don't really give a bucket of monkey jizz about them. Those who climbed out of the garbage can of life, flicked the shit bits off, and made something of themselves have my utmost respect.

Bulb

My mom used to tell me, "Wear clean underwear and socks in case you get hit by a bus." I think that if I ever got squashed by a bus, a skid mark in my shorts or a hole in my sock is likely the least lunch-regurgitating, nauseating thing the doctor is going to see when he's pulling a rib from my ear. Dad just told me, "Open your fucking eyes and watch where you're going!"

Bulb

I know countless millionaires and multimillionaires and a couple of lotto winners, musicians, and actors but not one PhD aside from doctors and dentists. Huh?

In-Th

Note to self: Peeing off your deck into your neighbor's flower bed is *not* the recycling they were talking about. Whoops. Sorry, Wilson.

B.M.

People who are unable to motivate themselves must learn to be content with mediocrity no matter how impressive their talents are.

Bulb

I work for a living because turkey dinners and hot tubs don't come free.

TFUW

Fucking shitty reality television, *America's Got Talent.* "I worked so hard to get here!" Yeah, you drove to the mass audition, stood in line with a thousand other wannabes, got a number, ate a granola bar, and sang a rendition of "Chipmunk Love" after the green-haired dork did an air guitar solo. Yup—work ethic right up there with going to war.

Bulb
Driven to succeed doesn't mean your mommy gave you a ride.

In-Th
Flea markets … The name? 'Nuff said.

Bulb
Only in our little corner of paradise in Canada is a neighbor mowing his grass one day and the next shoveling eight inches of snow. (Written November 6–7, 2020.)

LFBF
Is Tetris level 92 required of Costco cashiers and baggers? Until they make it that far, they're forced to be super-useless security people pretending to check receipts?

B.M.
If a clock tells you when to do something, you are your own slave.

T.S.
If you want to fix the world, never take the innocence from a woman or a child or the pride from a man. Do this and the world will start self-righting again. And yes, I'm being sexist, but I still hold some of yesterday's standards in high regard.

LFBF
Was it disco music that created so many serial killers in the seventies and early eighties?

TFUW
In a preview of some true-crime show on TV, some shithead said, "The people were drowned while they were still alive." How the fuck do you drown someone who's dead?

Bulb

If the restaurant you're eating in offers any kind of Jell-O dish for dessert, you have a better than average chance of eating a main course that was cooked in the microwave … Just saying.

WTF

What the fuck is Groundhog's Day, and how starved for any distraction from their shitty lives were the people who created the lame tale of a fat, dirt-dwelling rat seeing a shadow and shortening winter?

Bulb

Waiting on tomorrow likely means, "Wow! Did you fuck up today? And that was an ice cream sundae compared to the day before."

B.M.

We all get to decide what actually exists in our lives.

In-Th

Fuck. I just emptied the last of my bottle of good stuff, and all I have left is that cheap shit I give to annoying guests I want to go home.

Bulb

Standing still is for trees and kids playing hide-and-seek.

Bulb

I wrap birthday and Christmas gifts like I dance or menstruate—incredibly poorly or not at all. And FYI, I think cards are among the stupidest things possible, some cornball phrase or saying written by some semi-literate hack who likely splits his time between bong hits, Dungeons and Dragons, and searching for an internet bride.

LFBF

Why is the first day we call summer also the day that the days start getting shorter?

Bulb

I learned long ago that worrying is like a rocking chair; it gives you something to do but doesn't get you anywhere.

B.M.

The secret to life is making sure whatever road you're on actually leads somewhere worth going to.

TFUW

It's a fucked-up world we live in when the news has to sanitize all their opinionated stories and you have to bribe the garbage man to take the cardboard that the recycle guy missed. (At least maybe the latter can put it toward a new toothbrush.)

Bulb

There should always be a next chapter at the very least being brainstormed about at all times. No excuses.

T.S.

Family vacations and road trips when we were kids involved driving hundreds of miles to visit relatives, no seatbelts, no A/C, AM radio, Mom and Dad smoking in the front, and pee breaks were Mom holding a pickle jar as Dad passed semis trying not to squirt it all over the windows or my sleeping, car-sick brother. Yeah … What wasn't to love?

B.M.

Being altered by anything allows you to see and feel things on a level reality can't or won't give us the freedom to. It likely shaves years off also, so choose your path wisely.

LFBF

What big, floppy cock thought 2020 didn't suck enough? "Hey! Why don't we bring back the Spice Girls and that special-ed vampire crap from a decade ago?"

Bulb

I think Russell the garbage man used to find his own lunch every day at work.

Bulb

The TV show *Game of Thrones* broke firsts for many. It was the first time I saw a dragon on TV or in the movies, and for many basement-dwelling D&D nerds and various Pokémon champions, it was surely the first time they saw boobs other than their mommies'.

TFUW

An outline of a ring in the back pocket of teenagers' jeans used to mean they carried protection they likely weren't ever going to use, but today, it means they have one of those lazy buttons holders on the back of their cell phones for taking fucking selfies.

LFBF

Is the saying "beating around the bush" supposed to sound as dirty as it does?

In-Th

Anyone listening in on our phone conversation likely perked right up when I was talking to my brother earlier. He asked me to ask my wife (who owns a salon) what the strongest bleach and/or peroxide was that she could find because he had bones and a skull he needed to dunk right away.

LFBF

I'm curious about what the number of shots is that makes me legally impaired because it's usually about two or three before the creative, juicy insights get flowing, four or so before I start feeling the effects, and about nine or eleven or more before my writing turns into what the dogs do in the backyard.

T.S.
I write things like "Cub Scout Parts" and "Mailman's Ribs" on freezer-bagged steak, chicken, and pork just to fuck with people who snoop around in our refrigerator.

Bulb
Your career as a chef may be in the toilet if you went from being a celebrity chef with your own show on TV to someone who puts his or her name on gourmet dog food. But all is not lost if you're willing to work at Olive Garden or Red Lobster.

B.M.
Driving is like menstruation; only about half of any society is capable of doing either.

$$$$
Make waterproof, stick-on bull's-eyes to go in urinals that when whizzed on dissolve into that blue goop disinfectant and flush the toilet cake industry.

Bulb
TikTok is a six-year-old's artwork up on the fridge for adults—"Look what I did!" and equally sad to look at.

B.M.
Small-minded people always have too much on their minds.

LFBF
Is being buried at sea a euphemism for shark food or future whale turd?

B.M.
Kill the horse fast or set it free; just don't force it to plow twenty years of rocks and shit.

Bulb
Charmin butt wipes are like using a washcloth to clean your ass crack, and if you use more than two or three squares, it's like trying to flush a tablecloth or bedspread.

TFUW
Why the hell are airlines allowed to add absurd charges for shit like fuel, baggage, and airport fees? That's like ordering a pizza and hearing the kid on the other end of the line saying, "That'll be $12.99, but there's a $3 each surcharge for cheese and sauce and an extra $1.98 for crust."

WTF
In what world do those twenty-five-year-old, first-time home buyers on *House Hunters* seem real? "I volunteer at a shelter for sick ponies; I read them poetry and feed them organic, conflict-free apples, and my husband works as an artist repurposing old soup cans and used diapers. We're looking for a four-bedroom house with three bathrooms, large yard for doing goat yoga and monkey meditation, and a three-car garage not for cars but so we can build bicycles from straw and pine cones. We can spend up to $800,000."

B.M.
Fully grown or all grown up has nothing to do with height or weight.

Bulb
Shortcuts often look fun and fast, but more often than not, they lead straight into a brick wall.

T.S.
None of us will be around forever. Some will be missed, and sadly, others won't even be noticed.

TFUW

Days gone by, old guys who had gone to war told stories about the shit they had to do and see, but most of them had much deeper, darker stuff buried deep down that they didn't share. My generation was the last to do off-camera stupid shit that the current generation can't fathom. Kids of today will someday share their stories of youth about what? Playing Mario Kart? Wearing a helmet to walk down some steps? Playing a sport that no one kept score for? Getting top grades in a school that didn't allow anyone to fail? Future stories are going to be as interesting as porridge.

List 1
People Who Have Changed the World

- **The Wright brothers**. Invented flying. Air Canada would later find a way to turn their flying experience to shit.
- **Dr. Charles Drew**. Invented life-saving plasma. (I saw it on *M.A.S.H.*)
- **Steve Jobs**. Invented the smartphone, the prick! Now, everyone walks around with their faces buried in them like fucking zombies.
- **Philo Farnsworth.** He found a way to keep people at home and saved the world years later during the coronavirus outbreak of 2020. Look him up.
- **Daniel B. Wesson and Horace Smith**. Built one of the best and longest-lasting products almost two hundred years ago and continues to do so today. Ask Clint.
- **Adolf Hitler.** Obviously, he's currently burning with a volcano shoved up his ass in a special ring of hell reserved for political dickheads, pedophiles, and people who invite you over for dinner only to feed you a kale salad with fish, but he did at one time open the world's eyes to how shitty some are regardless of what others want you to desperately believe.
- **Henry Ford.** Made cars affordable for the masses and then later created the Edsel and the Pinto for the stupid with no taste.
- **Percy Spencer.** He turned the fine dining experience into a 7-11 burrito.
- **Tim Berners-Lee.** Gave birth to a world-sized army of know-it-alls who in fact usually know very little without him.
- **Thomas Edison.** If he hadn't stolen the idea of the light bulb or created the storage battery, we'd likely all be in the dark and Musk may have ended up working the drive-thru at Starbucks.
- **Elvis.** Otherwise, we'd still be stuck listening to shitty, boring, Gospel, Big Band, and operatic music.

✦ **Ronny fucking McD.** If clowns weren't scary enough, this guy has indirectly contributed to more deaths than all the serial killers combined in a way similar to the way Charles Manson used to pretend he had nothing to do with the Tate and LaBianca murders.

✦ **Mary Teresa Bojaxhiu, aka Mother Teresa.** She was known to have said something to the effect that suffering was a gift of God. She also was said to have an estimated net worth in the millions.

✦ **Princess Diane.** Since her untimely death, countless now ask, "What the hell does the royal family actually do?"

✦ **Clint Eastwood.** The godfather of the spaghetti Westerns who subsequently made a myriad of movies since depicting people who needed to stand up for themselves first and foremost instead of bitching and whining to everyone about their problems.

✦ **Justin Bieber.** Just kidding. I doubt he could change even a diaper.

✦ **Osama bin Laden.** This guy fucked up air travel for everyone even worse than Air Canada did as he was more international. Before him, you could stuff live land mines, Freddy Krueger gloves, and hockey skates into the overhead compartment as long as they fit, and your shitty meal came with real silverware. Now, airports treat a bottle of water like it's a vial of anthrax.

✦ **Mickey Mouse.** A talking rat on steroids created by a racist guy who's now the hallmark for amusement parks and cartoons all over the world.

✦ **Facundo Bacardi Masso.** Creator of the original rum we drink to this day. He took his inspiration for the bat logo from bats that flew above the original vats of rum knowing most couldn't read the label but would recognize the bat logo. The family still runs the business and now owns a large number of the most popular alcohols on the market today including Grey Goose vodka, Dewar's scotch, Martini & Rossi vermouth, and Patrón tequila but as yet no grappa. (I did have to look this guy's story up the next day when I sobered up.)

→ **Theodor Geisel aka Theo LeSieg.** He's credited with coining the term *nerd* and is among the top ten best-selling authors of all time up there with the likes of Shakespeare and Agatha Christie having sold some 600 million copies thus far. His stories amused and scared the hell out of generations of readers. He also went by his most recognized name, Dr. Seuss. And FYI, he wasn't a doctor of jack shit, and he didn't like kids.

→ **Hugh Hefner.** If his first wife hadn't cheated on him while he was in the service and he hadn't taken out a loan against his house for $600, the empire, lifestyle, and legend he created might never have come to be. That and the world may never have gone from a lights-off society to what it became and continues to evolve. Hint: Hef deserves a lot more credit for changing the world than he ever got.

→ **Pablo E. E. Gaviria.** Had an estimated net worth of over $30 billion at his death in 1993 making him the richest criminal in history (politicians excluded). His contribution to changing the world came in how countless other countries and territories now govern and enforce laws that may not have ever existed without him. It is believed that upward of 15 percent of all American dollar bills still in circulation from the eighties still have trace cocaine on them thanks to Pablo Emilio Escobar Gaviria.

→ **Adolf (Adi) Dassler.** Changed and perfected the way mankind actually moved. No longer were we simply a heel-to-toe society. Jesse Owens, Ben Johnson, Michael Jordan, and LeBron James owe a great deal of their fame and fortune to this guy.

FOUR SHOTS

LFBF
Shouldn't long weekends and extended vacations be all about regaining mental acuity?

Bulb
I think my dog just had a sex dream as she started kicking like a kung fu master and started moaning. Now I'm not going to be able to sleep.

LFBF
The Village People ... Why?

Bulb
Small touch-screen computers made in Japan are good only for anorexics, six-year-olds, and bony-fingered people in the West.

T.S.
As teenagers, we used to tell our folks every other weekend that we were sleeping over at a buddy's backyard in a giant tent. His parents were pretty clueless. We'd go out and do stupid shit throughout the neighborhood all night.

One night, we found another kid from the neighborhood sleeping in a hole he had been digging all weekend. When he had gotten home from school on Friday, he told his parents he wanted a pool. He had fallen asleep out of exhaustion, and his folks forgot he was still outside when they passed out.

B.M.
Feed yourself, feed your family, feed those close to you, feed what you care about, and feed those in need and then the rest of the world. In that order. Everywhere. The world would become self-sustaining in no time.

In-Th
Wow … Squirrels and bulldogs really don't mix.

LFBF
Is a fat health minister or a stupid education MP proof that the systems are broken or just piss-poor decision making due to political correctness? That's not optics; it's horrific judgment.

Bulb
Regardless what game you play in life, make sure you're actually playing it and not just swearing at it from the viewing side of a TV.

LFBF
If a dog shits anywhere, lies in the sun, watches as you clean up his poop, tongues his balls, and waits for you to serve him dinner, who is really the master, and why would anyone want to be reincarnated as anything other than him?

B.M.
The only thing worse than being trapped in a memory is living with the fact that you never actually did anything truly interesting enough to need remembering.

T.S.
The real Hotel California was a spiritual experience for me.

TFUW

I just saw an ad for fast food with some senior citizen dressed like a southern Ricardo Montalban saying, "Break out the good china and tell the kids to wash up. It's time for Sunday dinner even if it's not Sunday." When did eating utility-grade, reconstructed chicken parts, week-old fries greasier than used-car salesmen, and diabetes drinks become Sunday dinner? And who eats that greasy slop off any china let alone good china?

T.S.

If your coffee costs you $6 at a cafe each morning, you either don't actually like coffee or shouldn't be mixing the caffeine with your meds.

Bulb

Suspicion and nervousness are God's way of saying you were ill prepared.

Bulb

My male bulldog is tougher and weighs more than most of these hip-hop dipshits.

LFBF

Why is Viagra in the shape of a football?

T.S.

One year, my mom (having never seem the movie franchise or taken us to any of them) dressed me as that sasquatch bear thing from *Star Wars* for Halloween by cutting a hole in our fuzzy brown bathmat and buying me a $1.96 mask from Woolco.

T.S.

The next year, my dad was in charge of the costumes, and as oil prices had crashed, he pulled a big black plastic garbage bag over my head, cut a couple of arm holes in it with his pocket knife, and wrote "2¢" on my chest.

Bulb

(I stole this from the *Mayor of Lakewood*, but it made me laugh.) I Purrell so much now that every time I take a piss, I actually clean the toilet.

Bulb

Lying down is for old, tired dogs and porn actresses.

LFBF

If money grew on trees, how many would be too lazy to work in their gardens?

TFUW

I got yelled at today to put a mask on as I went into a bank to use the cash machine. Oh, Jesse James, talk about being born at the wrong time ... (Written May 29, 2020, during the coronavirus outbreak.)

LFBF

Is naming your kid Garland or Myron or Raul secret code for *Fuck! She's pregnant!*?

Bulb

So many try to look outside the box not realizing the most useful tool is the box.

T.S.

In grade school, the toughest kid was nicknamed the Gooch. She could kick anyone's ass.

WTF

Ironic how all health care systems have strangleholds on how society now functions.

Bulb

The Fonz looked cool only because he hung out with dorks.

Bulb
The neighbor's kid is proof that the current educational system doesn't work.

LFBF
Why do designer jeans for men have no room for the bat and balls?

Bulb
I freely admit I should have been fired from almost every job I ever had. I am completely unemployable and useless when it comes to doing mundane tasks.

T.S.
Someone brought a roll of butchers' commercial-grade shrink wrap to a lake party that we wrapped around the outhouse when the party shithead went in. It was ninety-plus degrees outside, and no one was letting him out. To the best of my knowledge, he tunneled out.

Bulb
A hundred and ten calories in *light* beer? Beer is really training for fat guys.

LFBF
If banana republics are so backward in the way they do things, why do so many do-gooders want to retire to them?

T.S.
A coworker who drove everyone nuts (and was the boss's nephew or cousin or something) pissed me off for the last time one shift, so I ran up behind him as he answered the corded phone hanging on the wall at the customer service desk and wrapped packing tape around his head, the phone, and his glasses as he tried to run after me but couldn't due to the cord as he screamed into the customer's ear. I was trying to get him fired.

B.M.
The number 8 is twice that of number 3.

LFBF
Why do NASCAR drivers drive like bats on fire coming out of hell but speak slower than an old lady with a shopping cart in a crosswalk?

Bulb
Sugar-free candies, secondhand stuffed animals, a cousin's hand-me-downs, and so-called learning toys all but guarantee your kids in the future will stick you in a government-run physicality and forget about you.

In-Th
Thank God my wife was willing to peel the layers off the onion that is me.

T.S.
As kids, we used to bumper cars in the winter to get anywhere. Bumpering cop cars was the ultimate prize.

LFBF
Why are so many shitty, average realtors (not the rare good ones) and all politicos failed something elses?

Bulb
True rock gods can't dance.

In-Th
I think my male bulldog tries to get me in shit.

Bulb
Chuck Norris had to know what was coming …

TFUW
Dorothy, Alice, Puff, or any of the Smurfs would have never existed in today's world of Ritalin and Adderall.

Bulb
With half the world currently working from home, I have to assume there are a shitload more interoffice romances and a hell of a lot more people getting laid on company time.

T.S.
If a dog's life is seven years for every one of a human's, no wonder they're always excited to see you and want to go for a walk. They truly do appreciate time.

Bulb
B&R's house smells like dried jism and tears.

LFBF
Did they ever use kale to torture prisoners of war?

T.S.
I once filled a colleague's work vehicle full of potatoes and covered a different prick's personal van with maxi pads and tampons I soaked in countless bottles of salsa the night before.

WTF
As kids, we used to collect basketball hoops from driveway courts. What the fuck were we thinking?

LFBF
Is winning employee of the year in a fast-food restaurant the polite way of saying, "You fucked your life up, but hey, thanks for making great fries"?

Bulb

I ran into a guy I went to elementary school with. Wow. Did he peak early.

B.M.

Regrets are nothing more than failed attempts.

Bulb

Ads on YouTube and rust are the same as they both insult your eyes and inevitably get you to buy shit so you don't have to see either of them any longer.

LFBF

Which one is Spock? The bald guy, the Scottish dude, the black chick, the remote-controlled garbage can that beeps, the nerd with the original Bieber haircut and white bathrobe, whoever the fuck Indiana Jones is, the robot with the pointy ears, or the black-masked guy with the breathing problem? Ahhh, who gives a shit? Fucking sci-fi sucks.

T.S.

I once told the kid in charge of the famous Blue Lagoon in Iceland that I was Sigourney Weaver so my wife and I could skip the mile-long lineup and get in. Not only did he let us in immediately; we also didn't pay, and I got to keep one of the big fluffy robes.

T.S.

If the bulldog ever learned to talk, the world would have been all over Uncle Sammy.

Bulb

Hint to parents: If your kids work at Appleby's, Tony Roma's or 36 Flavors and are in line to become shift supervisors, they're likely not moving out until they're in their thirties, and you're not getting grandkids, or if you do, you'll be raising them.

B.M.
The busiest place on earth is between our ears.

LFBF
Are banks forced to hired brain-dead dipshits and start them out as tellers? I have three tellers I use only for this reason.

In-Th
The sudden death of anyone close is a gut punch that lasts for an extended period.

T.S.
My twenty-year-old motorbike is better company and in better shape than half the people I meet; it requires less maintenance and has less shit spewing out of it.

In-Th
Music shaped me and taught me to dream. A piss-poor education system inspired me to reach beyond the drivel we were taught there and not drink the Kool-Aid. And football took me to heights physically and mentally that at five-eight I never should have seen.

$$$$
Why does all toothpaste taste like mint? It's not the 1800s with kids getting a fucking peppermint stick as a treat from old Nels at Olesen's Mercantile. Create flavors geared to specific groups.

- 18–30 years old—avocado toast
- Soccer moms—Zinfandel
- 70 and over—cream of wheat
- 1–6 years old—snot
- 6–15 years old—chicken nuggets
- 15–18 years old—warm beer
- Teenage moms—Tequila/Jäger

- Business people—Shecky's (gigi)
- Angry old men—bacon
- 30–69 years old—????

Bulb

I'd like to throat-punch the prick who goes through the Starbucks drive-thru and takes half an hour ordering eight of that pink dragon unicorn shit or any other whipped-cream and sprinkle drinks just so he can look like king-ding-a-ling for his office.

LFBF

Does anger management work?

In-Th

If I don't stop now, four is going to turn into fourteen.

LFBF

What exactly is the orange sand in a box of mac and cheese, and where the hell is the cheese?

Bulb

If you can't fight or defend yourself like Steven Segal, Chuck Norris, or Paul Kersey from *Death Wish* can, here's a handy tip: If a cop tells you to stop whatever the hell you were doing, stop immediately and put your fucking hands up—'Nuff said.

Bulb

We have a decent world; it's just currently full of lazy fucks acting on dumb-shit advice and trying to blame others for their shortcomings.

TFUW

An Asian restaurant in Canada that my wife and I went to for breakfast told me my choice (off their menu), "Number four isn't for you. It's for Asian people" and I should just eat the white people food like bacon and eggs. They did make pretty good French and Mexican items but totally fucked up my Italian coffee. Also, their telling me I wasn't Asian enough for my first choice … Isn't that what racism is, or does it go only one way nowadays?

Bulb
If you have never been hurt by anyone or anything, you have never laid it on the line and are likely far too familiar with mediocrity.

LFBF
What the hell are we trying to teach kids with things like the Tooth Fairy? Some creepy pixie waits until everyone is asleep, sneaks into the house, steals the DNA from under the kid's pillow, drops the kid a couple of bucks to shut the fuck up about it, and then flees with a bag of countless other kids' teeth. And what the hell is this freaky chick doing with all these gross baby teeth anyway?

Bulb
Basing yesterday's actions on today's standards is proof that the world in general has less understanding and common sense now.

Bulb
The guys on the evening news every other night for murder or armed robbery or banging their neighbor's shih tzu or whatever who say, "I was turning my life around" really weren't.

B.M.
Every single person has a story; some just get stuck in a particular chapter and don't let go of it until the postscript notes and thereby miss the rest of what could have come of their lives.

In-Th
I hate being on a clock.

TFUW

Freedom exists only in our perceptions as today's reality is about as real as Bigfoot or Ogopogo.

LFBF

When historians look back at 2020, what will they say? It was the year of hoarding toilet paper, electing morons (Written October 17, 2020, before the US elections but knowing that regardless of the outcome, the statement would still stand), and the beginning of the end of actual freedoms? I'm guessing that if the world makes it another hundred years, they are going to be either laughing at us or hating us.

Bulb

The fastest way to become a self-made millionaire is to learn the things that others think they know but don't and then do what others can't or won't do. That and get a good pair of work boots and stay away from the $8 lattes and $14 avocado toast.

B.M.

The only time number two is ever considered valuable or important is when you're constipated or looking for the other roll of toilet paper.

T.S.

If you asked used-car salesmen or others with crappy, nowhere jobs why they worked there and they replied with a semi-pissed-off "Why do you ask?" I'd think you had your answer.

Bulb

The apple never falls far from the tree. No shit.

TFUW

The Chinese (or arguably the Japanese) have been able to bake a cookie with a paper fortune in it for at least a century. A French chef from the 1800s baked a hotcake with ice cream in the middle, but the local high-end steak place can't nuke a plate of taco chips and cheese without infusing wax paper to them and the plate and yet still want $20 for the blob of crap. Huh?

LFBF
Why do we *look* at our watches but *watch* a clock?

T.S.
I love my wife. She punches imaginary ghosts when she drinks, and the one time she decided to go shot for shot with me and a couple of my buddies (one of whom is nicknamed Mush, so you can guess how this would end up), she took two steps out of the club bathroom where Mush's wife was singing and puked right on my shoes.

TFUW
We may have learned two tons of dogshit in public school growing up with the odd and rare nugget, but compared to today's world, those nuggets were pure gold. Now, they're barely green nose nuggets. I picked up a $30 bucket of crispy chicken for dinner (You and your partner work twelve- to fourteen-hour days and then tell me about the gourmet meal you made). The local tax on it is 5 percent, but the till was down, so I told the eighteen-or-so-year-old kid working there that I owed $31.50 and handed him $35. It took him five minutes to find a calculator and ten more after to figure out that my change was $3.50. In today's world, you could rob anything manned by a twenty-year-old with a handwritten note and a three-digit math equation.

Bulb
I'm willing to bet those *Botched* doctor dudes would be cool as hell to hang with.

Bulb
"Let's do this thing!" is the battle cry of people who likely shouldn't.

Bulb

Peeing in the dark is really an outdoor sport.

LFBF

When did Hollywood stop trying? Do they think we in the real world all lick windows, eat paste, and struggle with spelling our names?

Bulb

Living in the barren tundra in the extreme dark north, Santa is the reason fossil fuel isn't going anywhere anytime soon. At least not until he starts sacrificing reindeer and burning used elf jocks in his boiler room. Stop lying to kids about both!

In-Th

I saw a guy yesterday step out of a Thai restaurant and hand his leftovers to a rummy. That just seemed cruel …

Bulb

Lightning strikes, and doors open. Both happen constantly, but many flinch when either does.

LFBF

Are theme nights at swinging clubs and orgies the original mass-spreader events?

TFUW

They remade that shitstain of a movie *Charlie and the Chocolate Factory* but not *Blood Sport*, *First Blood*, or *The Corpse Grinders* and blacklisted *Death Wish* within a month when the remake came out. Huh?

Gov't

Believing governments will take care of you in your time of need is exactly how they want you to see it—to pass your responsibilities and bucks to them out of blind faith. Wake up! You don't mean shit to them other than as a tax and labor source. Own your own actions, and drive your own destiny.

LFBF
Why do women have to kiss a frog to find their princes? Why not kissing turtles or goats, or eating veal, or squishing spiders?

Bulb
A career is something you work to get. A job is a stepping stone and a means to getting a career.

T.S.
Little known fact that won't mean anything to anyone thirty-five and younger: before *M.A.S.H.*, the nerd Radar was in a band with the first real Wonder Woman, Lynda Carter.

LFBF
Why are aliens so obsessed with butt probes? What anal knowledge do they have that we don't?

B.M.
The night belongs to the willing, the disenfranchised, and the fucking wack-jobs.

In-Th
Tonight is not going to end at five …

LFBF
Do billionaires ever watch that dogshit *Who Wants to Be a Millionaire* and just giggle until they pee?

Bulb
Get lost in a foreign land and you will find salvation and your true character within.

T.S.

The only people who will ever order light roast espresso are hipsters in nerd socks and people who don't like espresso.

LFBF

Are the self-absorbed assholes who can't park at a coffee place somehow related to the morons who order Skip the Dishes for a fucking ice cream cone?

WTF

Yesterday …

Me: "Good morning. I'd like to make a payment on my wife's account please."

Britney the cashier (BTC): "Do you have her card?"

Me: "No, but this is our phone number that it's under."

BTC: "Okay. Do you have ID to match the name on the account?"

Me: "It's my wife's account."

BTC: "Ohhhh, then I'm sorry, sir, I can't do this for you."

Me: "What the hell are you talking about? I'm giving you money to pay it, not buying shit on it."

BTC: "Sorry, sir, we're not allowed."

Me: "Please get me your manager, Britney."

BTC: "My name's Kari, not Britney, but okay."

Me (after explaining to the manager and Britney getting permission to take my money followed by her standing there totally confused): "If anyone ever comes in and wants to pay for me or my wife or anyone else, fucking let them!"

Damn. Our world is a mess and full of real walking dead zombies …

$$$$

As every meeting, class, and seminar is now doing countless lame webinars, find a way to make cheap, life-sized, custom, human cardboard cutouts that move and blink.

T.S.

If you do half a job, you and I will never work together, but if you do half the work to get the job done and it's correct, I'll likely give you a raise.

Bulb

I applaud those willing to stick their necks out and go after any kind of business, but I saw a sign today that read "Slanted and Flat Roof Repairs Only." Maybe stick to what you're good at (and promo may not be it). By the way, what other kinds of roofs are there?

Bulb

Apple watches are this generation's bow ties.

In-Th

Buy Larry's house when he sells it to move closer to his grandkids and turn his backyard into my own lake with a guesthouse.

Bulb

Noshit, you don't have the coronavirus from your housebound four-year-old. You have a borderline neurosis of germaphobia brought on from smoking too much weed. Hell, you even wear rubber gloves when you're smoking it.

B.M.

If you somehow find that special place for you in life that can take all the ugly, everyday shit out of your head even for a little while, find a way to make it permanently yours regardless if it's a place, person, thought, song, or even a smell.

WTF

I thought I'd help out and do a load of wash and then fold the laundry. Fuck ... Are women's clothes complicated. Men's clothes require just folding them in half or rolling them up and dropping them off at the dry cleaners.

TFUW

Some dumpster-fire TV executive decided to put a disclaimer about nudity on before the show *Naked and Afraid* starts.

T.S.

I used to work with a guy whose wife we called Nut Cracker. She thought it was because of her love for Christmas, but he knew it was because she bitched him out over the phone in front of us on more than one occasion. Joke was on both of them as he hadn't had any nuts since the day he'd met her.

Bulb

Dollar Store finds last longer on the shelf than off it.

LFBF

As kids, we were told that we lost some 90 percent of our body heat from our heads, so we'd wear a toque when we went outside in the winter. I recall a teacher starting a clothing drive for hobos. I got sent straight to the principal's office after I asked, "If we really do lose so much heat from our heads, why don't we just get them those hats with ear flaps, a bottle of Sneaky Pete, a Big Mac, and a roll of one-ply and be done with it?"

Bulb

TicTok is, like, the first time you saw a pair of novelty socks. It was interesting, but by the time you've seen either for the sixth time, they all start looking the same and about as interesting as dental floss.

Gov't

Governments and politicians knowingly create division and animosity under the pretext of equality and egalitarianism to show the masses the value they seemingly bring to the table and thus make themselves look better while distracting attention from their inability to get anything done.

TFUW

A rep of a major fund company trying to impress me in hopes I would do business with him said to me, "We may not have the best-priced products or the strongest performers, but we are very competitive in the market." Perfect. Who wouldn't want to hear me say when they asked me why I chose this company, "Oh, I picked them because they're very average"?

In-Th

I know deep down that I'm capable of earning many, many millions more. I've been dragging my dick in the dirt for far too long … I'll do better.

B.M.

Passion burns only in those who give a damn about something.

List 2
Top Ten Positive Things about the Coronavirus Outbreak

10. Ugly Amish beards have started to replace ugly Duck Dynasty beards.
9. The doomsday prepper found in everyone's neighborhood looks less psychotic.
8. Fewer morons on the road driving eighteen km/h trying to figure out if this is where they need to turn left or if it's sixteen more blocks up.
7. Confused trendy masses no longer buy Corona beer thus driving down the price in the liquor stores.
6. Your stock in Newfoundland's Screech Rum may now be worth something.
5. The guy in the office who doesn't own soap now works from home.
4. As media around the world are now consumed with every little facet and trivial part about the virus, there are next to no filler stories about Bieber or the Kardashians.
3. Fathers everywhere now have a believable go-to story about why they can't take the family to the lamest place of earth, Disneyland.
2. No longer will anyone get awkward hugs from the office weirdos.
1. You can now tell dipshits to get the hell away from you with anatomical specifics and have total impunity.

FIVE SHOTS

LFBF
Why do so many alleged healthy vegans look closer to death than everyone else?

B.M.
Shouldn't those who hit signs with their cars take that as a sign?

WTF
Someone on TV just said, "It's been proven scientifically that when you dance, you can't be sad." What a chunk of horseshit! If I'm dancing, everyone is nothing but sad, both me emotionally and those watching me.

Bulb
Four to eight shots is the golden zone.

LFBF
If Death decides who gets to keep playing and who gets permanently benched, then is he the ultimate life coach or just an average referee?

Bulb
Hardest lesson for almost anyone coming of legal age *is two before nine and nine after two.*

In-Th

My beautiful wife was watching some reality TV crap *Dancing with the Stars*. I didn't have the heart to tell her that the only way anyone was going to see stars was if they fell off their couches and hit their heads.

LFBF

Does God hate assholes, or does he create them?

Bulb

Drive, desire, and effort are the trifecta of the qualities most sought after by any employer.

Bulb

Amicable divorce? How? You did something wrong.

Gov't

No real degree of success has ever been found in a government handout.

Bulb

Tequila is a six-year-old's Indian burn compared to the burn you get from a good grappa.

LFBF

Is Uber German for

  A) "Professional driver who can't drive,"
  B) "Car stinks like $8 worth of urinal Drakkar," or
  C) "If it wasn't for GPS, we'd never know where the hell we were."

T.S.

I and a couple buddies bought some cookie molds and three or four boxes of chocolate laxatives and melted them down in food class, wrapped them up, and gave them anonymously to our principal for Christmas back in high school.

TFUW
Dogs can tongue themselves and get humans to pick up their shit. Humans now eat kale salads instead of steak, drink vitamin water instead of alcohol, wear fucking pink shirts and man buns instead of suits and ties ... No wonder Clint always seems so mad nowadays.

T.S.
I knew I had made it when I had my own health advisor who made house calls, a pool guy, and a bullet maker. I knew I was Canadian when they all charged me only a few percent over cost in return for my help with their businesses and investments.

Gov't
In the States, criminals run south to the Mexican border, but in Canada, they don't need to because we keep giving criminals two, three, up to nine chances. Huh?

LFBF
Why are car ads 10 percent vehicle and 90 percent story about driving up a mountain to find a lost dog, or a date night, or babysitting the neighbor's brat kids, or something equally lame? Are the new cars so shitty that they need to distract us?

Bulb
Technology and mass immigrations are two of the biggest contributors to the destruction of ALL cultures.

$$$$
Make underwear with a brown strip the next trendy fashion statement.

Bulb
Shitty drivers will always be shitty drivers no matter how many dumb-ass assist gadgets car companies add to them. By adding these widgets, they are in fact making shitty drivers dependent on them, and they then drive even worse in normal vehicles.

Bulb
Michael's is the lonely nerd hut for weirdos ever since Radio Shack imploded from selling dork shit.

LFBF
If pink now means "Stand up to bullying," does neon green mean "Please go ahead and kick the shit out of me"?

T.S.
When I turned sixteen, my dad took me to his buddy's place to buy a car bigger than our school bus. I didn't.

Bulb
"The grass is always greener on the other side of the fence" especially my fence because the kid on the other side never picks his fucking weeds or waters what's left of his brown, dogshit-covered grass.

In-Th
I am always terrified when I eat grapes; I wash the shit out of them in 100 percent lit places. Being bitten by a black widow spider and consequently being hours away from losing my left arm was not an experience I care to repeat.

TFUW
Scented candles have about 30¢ worth of additional shit in them over normal candles but cost eight times more. Huh?

Bulb

God was either a joker or a brilliant planner. We all get less attractive as we age, but our eyes get worse, and we usually learn to grow thicker skin so it doesn't really bother us as much.

B.M.

Every single person will eventually go through some sort of period of self-abuse for one reason or another. Some are just better at it than others and stay there longer.

LFBF

Is it safe to assume that women who find a bed of roses romantic have been pricked a lot?

B.M.

Throwing up is far more interesting than throwing darts especially when someone else is doing either.

TFUW

Greta, shut the fuck up! Someone get her a Barbie!

Bulb

The only safe place on the internet while drinking is YouTube.

In-Th

McD's brings out the worst in me, both in the drive-thru and later in the bathroom.

Bulb

Those who think they must stop and eat at prescribed hours or sleep at specific times will never find fatty-wacker success.

LFBF

If cats could talk and had thumbs, would they be considered just another parasitic, lazy relative mooching off us?

Bulb

Dr. Phil and that other plastic-faced doctor guy are about as interesting as potatoes.

$$$$

Get the foreign rights to sell Viagra under the street name Bang-Long.

In-Th

I'm blessed with great neighbors including 3D (Double-Dipping Dean), Rich, Dr. Dave, Fishbelly, Larry, Puggy-Two Beers. Even GCB (Garbage Can Brian) is semi okay if I'm in a good mood and his loud kids haven't pissed me off in the last couple of hours.

Bulb

Observation: many cowboys walk like the horse rode them. Huh?

T.S.

I once almost bought a Ferrari (when I got super fucked up one night on grappa) off one of those online auction sites I suspect because I watched an old classic episode of the original *Magnum P.I.* earlier that night. I was, thank God, outbid in the dying minutes by a few hundred dollars.

LFBF

Do hardcore racists own only black-and-white TVs?

In-Th

Note to self (don't write this): Kick the first guy who asks about whatever awards show was on last night right in the purse.

????

A bulldog with three legs and no teeth is still more valuable than a pansy in a pot.

LFBF

Does working for the weekend mean you really can't afford it?

Bulb

Michael J, you were weird as hell and weak, but I did get it; fucking mental monkey chatter once started rarely stops.

WTF

Why are there fucking seagulls in every McDonald's parking lot in every landlocked prairie province?

B.M.

The man without a carrot is the donkey.

WTF

Why are drugs and alcohol regulated but fast food and reality TV aren't?

TFUW

There's a commercial on TV of a bulldog pulling a semi with a warning: "Teddy is a stunt dog. Don't try this at home." Seriously? What special-needs ad exec thought, *Better safe than sorry ...*?

LFBF

Why would you speed if you were driving a stolen car?

T.S.

My wife has great taste (obviously). Before she learned English, she picked one of the greatest, unknown, one-hit wonder songs of all time.

$$$$

Give some kid in a leather jacket $100 to drive around town in a big, old, piece-of-shit pickup that pukes black smoke and ask some tree-hugger vegan where the best barbecue restaurant in town is and get it on video!

Bulb

The name Justin likely came from scared fathers who thought, *Just-in case he's not mine.*

LFBF

How many modern doctors are closer to drug dealers than men of science? I'm guessing three out of five, and I'm lowballing that.

In-Th

I miss my long hair. I still have all my hair, but now, I'm too old, and it's grey, and I would just look creepy … At least I'm not Mark bald.

Bulb

A protest is the least angry way of admitting some form of failure.

T.S.

A rich little shit we went to high school with used to drive a Porsche and look down on the rest of us until one night we poured a bottle of moose piss we got from the local hunting shop in its open sunroof. Never saw much of him or his car after that.

LFBF

Can my buddy Cam be fined or sued for calling the kids he hires for his restaurants the real Walking Dead to their faces?

Gov't

Being a 100 percent socialist in a capitalist society means never moving forward.

Bulb

If TV screens and computer monitors could see and talk, most would throw up and then ask to be put in the witness protection program.

LFBF

If people smile when they fart silently, is that secret code for "Fuck you"?

Bulb

Kindergarten teachers should be watched very closely and potentially neutered.

In-Th

I have outlived a lot of people who were in every way better than me; 2020, you have been hard on the true old warriors. RIP Duly, Francesco, Molly, Ed … Next couple years, take some of the dipshits instead.

LFBF

Why does it take some almost dying before they started actually living?

T.S.

Hedgehog Frank was the only professional who lived in our neighborhood growing up, and he always waited until it rained to go outside and wash his car with the free water. He was a fucking lawyer.

Bulb

Pickles and ice cream for women is synonymous with being pregnant, but if you're a man, it just means you're a slob. It's very sexist.

TFUW

In what world is a fucking food blogger calling a restaurant out considered news, and how slow was that news day that they put it on the evening broadcast?

LFBF

If four out of five dentists recommend a specific toothpaste or gum, does that mean they couldn't afford the fifth one?

Gov't

Shouldn't politicians who would be fired in the real world be held accountable for the stupid things they do or don't do while in public office also?

In-Th

A .44 Bulldog? What the fuck were you thinking, Berkowitz? Oh ya ... Forget it. Never mind.

B.M.

The ability to work and earn is what allows someone to rise above those who won't or can't.

T.S.

I once filled a dishwasher in an office I worked out of with that liquid shit you use in the sink and left because the guy in charge I was working with late was a total dick.

TFUW

Neck tattoos on someone old mean they're likely tough guys or have done some serious shit. On the necks of twenty-somethings, they're more likely to mean "Follow me to my vegan poetry reading about bicycles, cats, and plastic-free Tupperware."

B.M.

Don't have dinner at the house of anyone who owns a skinny dog.

Bulb

In the eighties, we actually looked forward to and watched ads—especially beer ads.

LFBF

Who was the first guy to glue a bunch of raincoats together and then light a fire in a wicker basket tied under them? I'm guessing it was a really nasty shithole of a mental institution he was fleeing from, and I bet if he had heirs, at least one was in a boy band in the nineties.

Bulb

TV is so shitty now that there's actually a show about people clipping gross toenails and another with some chick popping zits.

Bulb

Ass scratchers are closer to monkeys than underwear pickers.

LFBF

Where did all the Al Bundys go?

Bulb

Those who have experienced, traveled, or lived globally have an infinite advantage and understanding over those who know only their backyards.

B.M.

There is no success without sacrifice.

In-Th

If your wife starts talking cute to the pets, don't ask her if she's having a stroke. You won't be getting a BJ as a reward for showing you care.

T.S.

My idea of hell is elves singing nonstop gangster rap Christmas jingles, being force-fed kale and Jäger every half hour 24/7 with only one-ply toilet paper in a Filipino open-air outhouse and the only channels available are the Oprah network, the Learning Channel, the weather channel, and the parliament channel. Also you're forced to breed with one of the Lohans, Roseanne, or any of the trailer park people from that Honey Boo Boo thing while being allowed to pal around only with Rob Kardashian and Pauly Shore and having to share a toothbrush with Steve Buscemi, Russell the garbage man, and the Marlboro camel.

Bulb
The only good snake is on a pair of boots.

In-Th
Wikipedia is not a great source of accurate information.

LFBF
Why are people and characters like Scrooge McDuck, Mr. Burns, Gordon Gekko, and Thurston Howell all depicted as evil for having money? Why the hell do you think the people who created them actually created them? Hint: to make piles of money.

TFUW
I know people who have been directly impacted by Chernobyl, the Vietnam War, Ebola, the coronavirus, and the Berlin Wall coming down but not one knee-jerk protester. Huh?

Bulb
If your shit really did smell like roses, your body might be a little confused as to what it needs to keep and what it needs to dump thus making you in reality full of shit.

In-Th
All eighteen- to twenty-year-olds should be forced to stay in a Third World country for thirty days and live off $10 a day (likely double what the locals earn daily). Maybe then when they came home, they'd bitch and whine less about all the frivolous shit they currently believe to be life-altering.

WTF
Does it seem that the public now gets to choose which laws they follow and which ones they don't?

LFBF
Why doesn't that socialist leader from the southern South Pacific do her speeches in her native language and just whinny?

Bulb
Black times ahead. Was that offensive? Exactly the point I'm making. (Written October 23, 2020.)

B.M.
Rare are those who can and do.

LFBF
Does YouTube assume you'll be drunker the longer you watch?

Bulb
Don Quixote could have saved Frankenstein from the protestors burning him out of the windmill if he hadn't gone batshit crazy from insomnia. That and if they had been in the same book.

TFUW
Desire and drive are now almost as rare as natural redheads in India.

Bulb
The trick to being remembered is having more defining moments doing cool shit than moments doing nerdy shit. FYI, if tough-guy shit ever goes out of style, the world will be lost and everything will mean nothing, so put a bucket on your head, jerk off into a watermelon, and write some poetry about clouds.

B.M.
Crackheads with PhDs are truly gifted.

LFBF
Seriously, who decides?

T.S.
Guys with nice bikes who can't ride make me sad.

In-Th
I found it incredibly difficult to find anything that fit in the land of sumos (Tokyo, Japan). Should I be concerned? I'm five-eight and 220 but take a size 48–50 suit jacket and a 36 pair of pants.

Bulb
My neighbor Barb says I paint with words. If you asked my wife, she'd say I have to because when I use a brush, my actual paintings resemble what babies do in their diapers.

LFBF
"What's good for the goose is good for the gander." Who the fuck cares? Which one tastes better with a lemon glaze?

T.S.
The quality of villains has been in a sharp decline since the days of Rowdy Roddy Piper.

Bulb
No one ever asks me and my wife to babysit. My brother did once, but I lied and told his kids it was almost midnight at 5:30 p.m. and put them to bed. The next morning, I taught them a couple of dirty nursery rhymes and fed them eight pounds of sugar an hour before he picked them up. The kids seemed happy. Huh?

LFBF
Do porn stars ever go meet a friend for a coffee after work and say, "I just came from work"?

In-Th
Correct grappa rhythm is 15:1, but by the sixth shot or so, it's often way out of wack beyond that.

TFUW
Everyone is talking about the coronavirus vaccine and getting life back to normal instead of taking this as a lesson and moving forward. "Back to normal" is people bitching about songs like "Baby It's Cold Outside," pseudo celebs promoting $80,000 purses, and hospitals full of people with bagel-related injuries. (Written December 11, 2020.)

Bulb
Life comes with multiple chances in the same way a gun comes with multiple shots, but if you blow through either without first readjusting, they will produce the same shit results over and over.

T.S.
My wife and I have traveled the equivalent of circumventing the globe several times over and on our own nickel ... Not bad for someone my high school guidance counselor wrote off and deemed would amount to half a pile of elephant shit.

Gov't
Our prime minister has all the ethics of an alcoholic being put in charge of the sacramental wine or a pedophile running a daycare.

TFUW
For the love of whatever you love, Hoff, take a page from Ricky Martin and hang it up already before you accidently do another embarrassing

floor-sandwich video again. Oh, wait … Too late. You just sung lead vocals for some German heavy metal band. Fuck, dude!

LFBF

My neighbor, 3D, made a great point the other day. Why do they have traffic helicopters? You're not watching the news at work before you go home, and once you're there, what the hell do you care about traffic conditions?

Bulb

If you have to ask, "Was that a compliment?" it wasn't.

In-Th

I live a very blessed and tranquil life for the most part. I have one buddy who actually goes to the gun club for peace and quiet.

T.S.

Until society decides to point the finger at the real problems and stops band-aiding whatever the flavor of the day is, nothing will ever actually change.

TFUW

I drove past some promo for a gas station today that read, "Go carbon-free with …" It was written over a background of a lush, green jungle. I wonder if the marketing genius behind this knows what photosynthesis is.

Bulb

The difference between men and women is that many men try to bang women's assholes and women far too often end up being banged by assholes.

LFBF

Does Jesus get Christmas or birthday gifts on the 25th?

Bulb
Society works only if everyone plays by the same rules and if those who don't are held to the same standards of accountability.

T.S.
Lemmy gave me the best drunken advice I ever got, but I hardly understood four words he said.

WTF
Here's a handy little tip for the sponge-kid generation and the teachers doling out half-info thereby confusing that generation: The planet has and always will be going through climate change. It isn't something new brought on by hair spray and old Pintos. Fuck, I come from the frozen north part of Canada, and at one time, we had palm trees and dinosaurs there.

B.M.
Many great artists live their lives in dog's years.

TFUW
Originally, I assume they called it fast food because you got your meal quickly, but nowadays, it's more because of how fast your tasty bag of greasy vittles turns to a cold, goopy blob.

In-Th
I have only a shot or two left in this bottle and several hundred insights so far. This seems like a fairly natural place to stop both.

In-Th
Fuck that.

T.S.
It's a pride thing for me that I treat everyone with respect until I deem them no longer deserving of respect. Then, all bets are off.

Bulb
Mental tears can scar but only if we let them.

LFBF
Was Ivan Drago's mouth guard made from an old tire he swiped off a Lada?

TFUW
My sister-in-law (in South America) wrapped a banana at Christmas and gave it to her kid as a test to see his reaction before she gave him any of his real gifts, and he was ecstatic to get it. Try that with your own kids here and watch their reaction and then tell me how we here in North America aren't spoiling our own world.

T.S.
Noshit got his nickname after a weeklong bout of constipation.

In-Th
Don't mix the grapes …

Bulb
Old-money mansions have the most closets with skeletons in them.

LFBF
Do you ever look at some people and wonder if the stork had the address wrong?

LFBF
Those crackers that look like little fish (for some dumb reason) just had an ad on TV that said, "They're as fun as goldfish." What the hell is fun about goldfish other than flushing them?

List 3
Top Ten Negative Things about the Coronavirus

10. Death for countless individuals, health care systems, and various economies around the world.

9. Guys who can't grow facial hair now look like sick cactuses.

8. As this becomes a global reset, everyone gets a second chance to start again and get out of life what they want, but most still won't take advantage of it because no one told them to.

7. If going to Costco wasn't a total shit-shoot, snake pit before, enjoy it now.

6. Gas may have been cheaper than a Dollar Store condom, but it's equally as useless as no one had anywhere to go.

5. Poor hair dressers and barbers everywhere are now stuck dealing with an onslaught of people who look like Cousin Itt from the *Addams Family* after each regional lockdown.

4. Pain-in-the-ass neighbors are blaring shitty trumpet and accordion music because some politico prick said to play it as a thank-you for essential workers who are either lucky enough to be at work and not hearing the god-awful countless renditions of "Blame It on the Rain" or are pissed off trying to sleep like the rest of us.

3. Starbucks drive-thru lineups now offer enough time for your choice of a Rip Van Winkle–length nap or enough time to knock out six and half years of back taxes.

2. As meat prices skyrocket and many try kale for the first time and consequently discover how shitty it tastes, once this is somewhat over, restaurants will stop trying to force it into every other entree. (Sorry. This is a positive thing if it actually happens.)

1. The things that may have been dealt the biggest death blow are hygiene, self-grooming, and overall appearances as so many now are becoming accustomed to working in their underwear with three-day-old bedhead and just pretending that their internet is wonky as a reason not to have their video camera on.

SIX SHOTS

Bulb
If you call yourself a specialist at something but can't do more than the average person practicing in your field can, you're not a specialist, you're just overpriced with a balloon-sized ego.

Gov't
Do career politicians get long-term health benefits because the vast majority are brain dead and need it?

B.M.
Our only regret in life should be what we couldn't do.

LFBF
If we all refused to pay all the ridiculous airline surcharges, would that mean we'd just sit on planes with no food and snotty service staring at a seatback because that would be still better than whatever Air Canada offers?

$$$$
Invent a diaper with an extra-large turd compartment for multi dookies. Same idea but in adult sizes for nights out after eating Thai food.

TFUW

TV used to be written about average, semi-boring people doing something interesting. The difference with today's reality TV is that they write story lines about boring people doing boring shit.

T.S.

In my youth, I once came home after a night out drinking with the boys and wanted another drink or two but didn't have any alcohol in the house. So I tried to make vodka by pulling out my juicer and tossing a bunch of potatoes in it. I puked violently, and my shit smelled like old potato peelings for a week.

In-Th

Drove by a scrapyard earlier today and saw Rusty's brother in it. Ahh, shit …

Bulb

If your pharmacist says, "Good morning, Mr. X. How can I help you today?" you need to change your lifestyle and fast.

LFBF

Cute as a bug's ear … What the hell does that mean, and what fuckwad wrote it?

Gov't

Trump may be a brilliant mind (in an empty room), but he's still light-years ahead of the train wrecks the Democrats currently have. Three hundred and fiftyish million Americans and these are their top choices for running a world powerhouse? I'll shut up. We re-elected a guy dumber than soup.

TFUW

High school dropouts used to form bands and live off pennies until they went bald and became music teachers, or did something that changed the world (as all those computer dorks did), or just fade away and die of obscurity. Not like today's world, in which some jagoff dropouts open organic hot dog restaurants for three days a week and then demand $250k from the government via social assistance only to find them six months later bitching to every media outlet they can find because they didn't get the support they wanted and they inevitably shit their business bed when their dumb-ass, adult Kool-Aid stand of an idea failed.

LFBF
Has anyone anywhere ever sat through an entire webinar?

B.M.
There is one face that will mock and show disappointment without ever changing expression throughout every man's life, and it's the same face for all of us.

Bulb
Fucking Costco. Went there today to buy four items, stood in line for forty minutes, spent over $500, rolled my ankle pushing that semi-sized flatbed cart, and forgot three of the damn things we went in for. I'm also guessing those two pieces of $1.25 heat-lamp pizza will wake me up and chase me to the toilet for a 3:00 a.m. stinkfest.

LFBF
If the moon was really made of cream cheese, who would have already have laid claim to it, France or Philadelphia?

T.S.
I empty the garbage from my car into B&R's mailbox every time I pick them up because they're both too hung over to drive. Done it for years, and they still haven't clued in.

T.S.

In junior high, we used to toss our PB&J Wonder Bread sandwiches, open juice boxes, and half-eaten fruit into the drop ceiling in the school to make the stink drive the principal nuts and to see whose shit lunch would make it eventually fall. It was kind of a kid version of a lottery.

Bulb

My favorite cafe is Timmy's. Just kidding. I like coffee that isn't made with hot water and a brown crayon. Blueberries Cafe in La Paz, Bolivia, Cafe Paris in Reykjavik, Iceland, and Cafe Pura Vida in Costa Rica.

Bulb

Someone pissed while camping who is willing to light the fire or chop wood is someone you should play poker with.

Bulb

There's a fifty-fifty chance that without GPS, an Air Canada flight would travel 9,000 km and somehow land at the same airport it had departed from without realizing it.

TFUW

During the coronavirus, when international travel was either highly discouraged or disallowed, the only language I didn't hear in one of our national parks in Alberta, Canada, was English. Huh?

LFBF

Is a wrecking ball a sign of change?

T.S.

I feel like Sheldon Cooper when I watch TV game shows.

In-Th

I have to stop pulling my mask so tightly or I'm going to end up with ears like Will Smith.

LFBF

What if Jimmy Hoffa had simply said "Fuck it" and left?

$$$$

Find a way to make farts smell like potpourri and crush the stink spray industry.

LFBF

Will the Village People eventually be one of the casualties of the "Defund the Police" movement because they had a cop in the group?

In-Th

Is it a conspiracy that the world makes stupid people famous for nothing extraordinary and still no one asks why?

Bulb

Western religion needs to do a major rethink. Muslim dudes will blow themselves to bits for a chance to hang with Allah and a bunch of virgins while all Western religion offers is a chance to be judged by some peace-loving dude in a bathrobe threatening to send you straight to hell if you don't obey his every thought. Maybe free, endless hot wings and drinks upon entering the pearly gates would be a good start. And lose the pearly gates for something less ostentatious.

LFBF

Which hurts worse—being kicked in the balls, being stabbed in the back, or having your head stomped on? Asking for a friend …

Bulb

Real guitar playing and air guitar aren't even distant cousins.

LFBF

Is the idea of all Charlie Church do-gooders (those who drive every-one else fucking nuts) going to heaven the reason most religions are in a major nosedive?

T.S.

At a party, we once tried to "feng shui" a couple of drunks passed out on the floor but just ended up tossing an area rug over them.

Bulb

The Skipper should have killed Mrs. Howell for her jewels, locked the Professor in a cave and forced him to invent shit for him, made Ginger and Mary-Ann his Mormon wives, stole the billionaire's booze and watches, and made Gilligan his idiot monkey butler.

Bulb

Grappa is both an excellent defunker and temporary memory wash with little to no hangover.

Gov't

Do governments now tell doctors and schools to pump kids full of Benadryl, Ritalin, and other happy shit to keep anyone of them from ever trying to be John Wayne again?

LFBF

Is having sadistic instincts a prerequisite for dental school?

T.S.

Clint and Clapton took different paths in life but shared a drive and commitment all but unknown nowadays.

????

I didn't read their names in the paper or see some crazy shit on the TV news, so I guess they're all right …

LFBF

Why are the people who get paid for all the Stat holidays usually the upper-middle to top management and are least deserving or in need of them?

LFBF

During the coronavirus outbreak in 2020, I was stuck outside the country and under martial law for weeks. I used the time to transcribe these thoughts from scribbles to book format and learned how to make alcohol while countless others just jerked off to Netflix and the Disney Channel. Which of us will they let inside the wall when the zombies and/or liberals attack?

Bulb

If you don't look for, find, or utilize your gifts, you'll have an above-average chance of becoming one of the sheeple-people.

B.M.

Truth always bites harder than fiction.

WTF

Why do all the twenty- and thirty-somethings on that reality crap about Americans getting married abroad to people they met on the internet take their fucking nosy parents with them to meet their internet love interests? Morons trying to reattach the umbilical cord. Grow a set, you fucking adult babies.

T.S.

I don't know how anything works anymore.

LFBF

Wanting what you can't have can make you dangerous, but having what you don't want makes you successful or lazy?

Bulb
The Monkees were the original Teletubbies.

Bulb
Orange sucks … The color *and* the fruit.

In-Th
Sergio, you and I are more alike than you realize.

LFBF
If food gets broken down and is eventually turned into shit causing it to stink like hell, why does barfed-up, undigested macaroni smell even worse?

$$$$
Vegan hair products that smell like tacos.

Bulb
Weeds will always overtake planted seeds, so we should learn to like the flavor of them.

B.M.
Being open minded works only when you open your mind and let go of your predispositions.

LFBF
How many famous people would be totally anonymous if it weren't for their publicists?

Bulb
Smoking may kill in, like, forty years, so it's frowned upon by many, but being too scared to live your life kills every single day and is accepted by countless numbers … Huh?

T.S.

One night, one of the biggest names of the nineties rock world kept telling everyone on Sunset Strip in LA that I was his bodyguard, and we got what I thought was ploughed. That was until I helped a different member of rock royalty, one from the seventies, up when he feel off the stage. After that show, I found out what drinking really meant.

Bulb

A $30 cigar and four shots at $6 each are still 8,000% better than blowing $50 on a damn Disney flick in a sticky theater.

LFBF

If you ate only ice cream and drank only slurpees every day, would you get used to that enough not to get a diamond-splitting headache before you died of diabetes?

LFBF

Is modern religion losing out because man's faith in God is being challenged by man's stupidity in reality?

????

After thirty-eight Tic Tacs, if someone's breath still smells like a bear's ass in summer, that equals a lawsuit.

Bulb

I saw another sign on a church today: "Don't ruin today by worrying about yesterday's problems." Morons, instead of sticking your head in the sand, how about finding a solution to today's problems so tomorrow doesn't suck?

????

Was Cap'n Crunch cereal originally invented to put sailors with scurvy out of their misery?

LFBF
When dipshits talk, does God laugh or cry?

Bulb
Cher's costume designer in the eighties either didn't give a fuck or was given a hell of a lot of leeway. Regardless, I'm betting he or she went to a fair number of love-ins in the sixties.

WTF
How scary is it that my drunk writing looks almost exactly like my doctor buddy's everyday writing?

LFBF
Who was that first penniless bastard whose wife said, "You need to pick something up to barbecue tonight for us and the neighbors" and ended up getting the ground-up, scrap cow bits from the butcher and then with the luck of a lotto winner after mushing it together into patties and covering it in condiments, it somehow tasted good? And how drunk was he when someone said, "Wow, Fred! This is delicious. What is it?" and he replied with a lucky dipshit's pride, "Ham-burger"?

Bulb
Spaghetti Westerns may have been corny by today's standards, but they still made more sense than avocado toast.

In-Th
Uncle Ju, thank you and Riccardo Cordiferro for "Core 'Ngrato."

Bulb
The number one program used by on-duty realtors, insurance agents, and finance people is solitaire.

LFBF

Is a clown who's not funny as big a failure as someone who tries to commit suicide and lives, or are they both piss-poor cries for help?

Bulb

The media's now a prostitute who doesn't take any clothes off.

Bulb

Anyone who has seen Death close up knows how ugly he is, and anyone who has looked him in the face more than once can see him in every mirror.

Gov't

Life is the ultimate casino, and death is the house that always wins, but for reasons unknown, the only one that gets to collect either way is the government.

LFBF

"Fart in a Can"? Didn't the original also come from a can?

In-Th

Like so many things in life, numerically, it could be considered by 1 to 3 as fighting through, 4 to 5 as warrior potential, and over 6 is realized success (entrepreneurially thinking).

Bulb

God or who or whatever you believe in blessed all of us, but fucknuts wanted something someone else had gotten in addition to whatever they got.

T.S.

I have been known to drink both events and some people until they become interesting.

Bulb

I'm betting Stompin' Tom would have been a pretty cool guy to have beers with, but by six or seven, he'd probably sound a lot like Popeye. RIP, Golden Dory.

In-Th

Sammy knows secrets about me and my uncle, and he's never met either of us.

LFBF

Why are things written in lipstick on mirrors always in perfect penmanship but all "honey-do" notes and lists come closer to doctors' writing in Sanskrit or Farsi?

Bulb

Fourteen feet is the magic point for several reasons. Retired ops living in shit neighborhoods get this.

Bulb

Current magic bullet for retirement is 300 + 10 x 20 (+/- 10 percent).

B.M.

If it works, work it until you or it is dead.

LFBF

What happens when the person giving a competency test is incompetent, and who decides?

In-Th

Remember to toss some peanuts into Wilson's yard so the damn squirrels will leave my fruit trees alone.

$$$$
"Defund the police"? Ya. Can't wait to see how that's going to turn out. Look into buying the *Death Wish* and *Dirty Harry* franchises before the resurgence starts.

Bulb
St. Valentine's Day, Black Friday, New Year's Day, St. Patty's Day, and Thanksgiving are all suckers' days.

TFUW
Walking in someone else's shoes can be very enlightening until you realize most people have the capacity to change them for better pairs but just don't.

Bulb
It always amazes me how dark it is under the bright neon lights and backstage.

LFBF
Do they dunk those baby ducks in oil for those dish soap ads? Because that's as cruel as someone inviting you out for dinner and then taking you to Olive Garden.

Bulb
The only thing that expunges pain isn't booze, drugs, or stupidity; it's willingness.

T.S.
I don't really care for rap or hip-hop or whatever it's called, but I do have to give some of those dudes credit. When it comes to self-promoting, they make Gene Simmons and NASCAR look like gofers at an ad agency in comparison, but how did that one guy get people to shell out $100 to buy a candle that supposedly stinks like him? That's top-shelf, impressive promoting.

Bulb
Secondhand items that should be avoided at garage sales and flea markets regardless of the price: diapers, Kleenex artwork, feminine hygiene products, clothing worn "south of the equator," German pornography, homemade booze, baked goods, bathroom readers, dental products …

WTF
Someone once said, "It's better to burn out than to fade away," but if you burn out before you actually accomplish anything, what the hell difference does it make?

LFBF
Why are there countless allergy medications to treat runny eyes, snot, and congestion but none to cure them?

Gov't
Running inside jokes is the basis for all governments.

In-Th
I bet back in his day, Shakespeare got his ass kicked a lot in school, the same as that Greek blowhard Socrates.

Bulb
You're fucked when staying is worse than going …

T.S.
The only free ride I'm willing to give whiners and crybabies is from the end of my boot.

LFBF
If your doctor smokes and drinks, does that make him more human or more hypocritical?

Bulb
Thunder and lightning are Mother Nature's way of saying, "Nice deck and nice garden party, but I'm still in charge, bitch!"

T.S.
I once called a city councilor a "balding bag of monkey spunk" to his face for bullshitting, but he still smiled nervously and tried to shake my hand because of a photo op. The fucking loser.

LFBF
What the fuck was wrong with Jim Hensen? Dude was a grown man sticking his hand up puppets' asses and pretending they talked.

B.M.
The smell of success is different for everyone.

Bulb
To much ice cream and chocolate leads to brain freeze, ridicule, and an early grave.

LFBF
I wonder how long it took to wake Joe and let him know he'd won.

Bulb
Skip the Dishes and Uber will never know my address.

In-Th
I think I saw Snooki in her latest and most promising role of working the drive-up window at a donut shop.

Bulb
Triscuits taste like cattle feed infused with herbs, onions, and tomatoes.

In-Th

I want an octopus army … Or would that be navy?

TFUW

A fridge with a TV built in would be rather expensive, so you'd have to be somewhat successful at whatever you do to afford one. But if you need TV so badly that you're going to be watching it by staring at your fridge, how successful could you be? Whatever … I'd be making fun of you for having one regardless.

LFBF

Are great chefs at vegan restaurants still considered to execute great meals?

T.S.

For reasons I don't really understand, my wife hides our toilet paper.

LFBF

At what phase of the reopening do terrorists and other wack-jobs go back to work?

Bulb

Our male bulldog has my wife wrapped around his finger, and the little shit doesn't even have fingers.

B.M.

There's usually a reason uniformed, unsolicited information is free.

Bulb

"I drove all night" will be replaced by "I Ubered until my credit card maxed out."

TFUW

Alexa is a needy, pretentious, chunk of shit! I have never had the displeasure of using her retarded and ostentatious sister Suri, and don't plan to. I wonder … Can I change her name to Britney?

In-Th

Milhouse (not the nerd cartoon but my real one lovingly nicknamed after him because he used to call me Lisa), you and your sister don't know it, but you both inspire me.

T.S.

At one time or another, I have had to wounded-warrior carry over my shoulder each one of our three bulldogs home from a walk when each decided it had had enough exercise for the day and were done and just lay down in the middle of the street.

Bulb

I didn't see a 3:00 a.m. helicopter in the park, so I guess Rich and Karen didn't win the fifty-fifty last night. Damn. So I guess I can take this cop uniform off now and go to bed.

LFBF

Was Popeye supposed to have had a stroke and an ambidextrous addiction to jerking off eight times a day? Because then he would have made sense.

TFUW

Political Correctness 101: Take the best hunters in the village out and get them to stay back with the old ladies and little kids making wallets and beaded necklaces because Herbie, the 350-pound nose picker, wants to try because he got three stuffed animals playing the water squirt game against a handful of eight-year-olds and can pick more berries than anyone else in the community garden and his mommy said he'd be great at it.

B.M.

Anything and everything can be weaponized and sadly eventually will be.

Bulb

You're not an outlaw-gangster if you're driving a station wagon with a baby seat and a "Bring Back Hillary" bumper sticker regardless of your do-rag and neck tattoo.

SEVEN SHOTS

B.M.
Anyone who gets help constantly is in actuality being killed slowly.

Bulb
Living Barbie dolls eventually look more and more like Mr. Potato Head.

$$$$
If McD's and the taco place with the talking rat dog can make the recycled phone books and the possum parts they call food taste good, why can't someone figure out how to make broccoli taste better than crunchy grass?

In-Th
Why is my go-to response to those I deem to be brain-dead, crayon-eating morons whom I can't get away from or shut up, "Go fuck yourself, you dipshit!"? Is it because I subconsciously don't want them to reproduce?

LFBF
Are old geezers called blue hairs because they stare at kids with blue hair?

Bulb
The world is full of Pinocchios thinking they're Gepettos and demanding to be treated like a Khaleesi.

TFUW

Will the game of pool one day be banned because it's racist? A white ball pushing every other colored ball off the big green surface?

????

Churches hurt. All of them.

LFBF

If drinking kills brain cells, does it opens minds by freeing up space?

Bulb

11:18 p.m. to 12:27 a.m. is typically the exact hour(ish) when my writing and thoughts start to become harder and harder to decipher.

Bulb

If eating kale was the key to longevity, I'd be dead by next September.

In-Th

What the fuck were my ancestors thinking moving to Freeze Your Dick Off in June Northern Canada? Oh wait … We moved back here a few years ago too.

Bulb

You are a true woods master if you can shit off the side of a canoe into the water and not get wet.

LFBF

Are Bernie Sanders and Joe Biden so angry because they can't buy Sanka anymore?

Bulb

The meaning of life is knowing when to shut the fuck up (STFU) and take shit from someone lesser so you can get on to the next play and not look back because they weren't worth your time or energy as you pass them by.

$$$$
Invent a canoe with a place to drop a steamer.

????
Henry the VIII had no follow-up, and he needed a fork.

LFBF
How crappy of a fisherman was the first guy to say, "I'm just going to eat the snot innards of one of these little black pincushions lying all over the ocean floor"?

TFUW
If the world wants to eliminate all hate, does logical, judicious thinking mean love would also have to be euthanized in the same way you can never be happy without knowing first what is sad?

Bulb
Life is a game of whom you know in hopes they'll fuck you over less than the ones you don't would.

LFBF
What the fuck does "silk purse–sow's ear" mean?

Bulb
I want my future casket to be made from mango trees.

WTF
How did Cadbury make chocolate and sugar taste so shitty, and what the fuck were they thinking making it jism-like creamy?

T.S.

I can drink three-fifths of a twenty-six-ounce bottle of grappa, solve a Rubik's cube, and never get a hangover the next day, but give me even two shots of rye whiskey and there's a better than average chance your refrigerator ends up in your front yard by morning and I likely won't even remember why or how it got there.

LFBF

Does Death work for the Devil or God, or is he an independent contractor?

B.M.

If palm trees could talk, they'd all be perverts.

Bulb

Tramp stamps date a person as much as being a fan of shitty modern or disco music does.

T.S.

I once took a shit next to the car of the deputy police commissioner of the Royal Canadian Mounted Police, RCMP—Canada's national police—because he was hogging the bathroom.

Bulb

The only place an activist takes precedence over work or ethics is in a dictionary, yet ironically, many knee-jerk activists have likely never held an actual dictionary other than the one on their phones they use to film themselves being activists.

WTF

What the hell were Jagger and Bowie thinking when they did that turd of a video "Dancing in the Streets"?

Bulb

Yesterday's partying all night and 4:00 a.m. greasy diners once meant a great night out, but now it means 260 pounds and heart disease.

In-Th

Either my shorthand sucks or many of my grappa thoughts are written in a language I can't read.

Bulb

Life really is passing you by if you stand there and watch the microwave tick down.

LFBF

Whatever happened to that kid in grade school who would eat dirt for a nickel?

T.S.

If you toss your underwear at a moving ceiling fan, it will short, it out.

Bulb

Stereotypes can be degrading and derogatory and even cruel, but they usually have a hint of truth.

$$$$

If cigarette ashes smelled like bacon or pastries, they'd be even more addictive and socially acceptable.

Bulb

George's retired neighbor is such a perverted prick that I think he may have been a priest.

LFBF

Today, does knowing geography without using an iPhone mean you're old? Being able to count and write a full sentence definitely seems to.

Gov't

The public sector does what is deemed acceptable. The private sector does what is actually wanted but beyond the reach of those willing to accept acceptable.

T.S.

I tried to sell a dead palm tree as a do-it-yourself grass hat kit at a neighbor's garage sale.

Bulb

Even those little skinny dudes who often found themselves locked in lockers in high school look cool in old muscle cars.

????

Every secondhand couch is seen as having naked ball prints.

Bulb

Snow is Mother Nature's way of saying, "Get the fuck out of here!"

LFBF

Do all men secretly see themselves as pigeons shitting on whatever they want to?

T.S.

One of the biggest advantages gay dudes have over everyone else is that they don't have to deal with *Shark Week* or *Uncle Bloody's* monthly visit.

LFBF

Is letting go of a bunch of balloons a snobby way of littering?

TFUW

Being rich once meant having what someone else wanted, but now, it means what someone else believes.

In-Th

If God is a cat, a politico, or actually likes The Learning Channel (TLC), I know where I'm ultimately heading, and I better start soon hanging out in the Caribbean more so I can get used to the heat.

Bulb

In every memory lives a childhood of innocence usually less than complete or accurate.

WTF

Aren't public libraries just places where the homeless go to sleep and bathe? Then why the fuck are there so many sexy stories on TV and in the movies about people getting laid in them?

T.S.

Fuck. I just drew on myself by accident for the third time.

LFBF

Who was the first guy who hated mankind so much that he put a worm in a bottle of booze? And what dumb-fuck tourist thought, *Wow! Cool!* and bought it?

T.S.

I used to take an old hockey stick and flick my eighty-pound bulldog's shit over the fence into my neighbor's yard (who had a three-pound Chihuahua pocket rat), and the only reason I stopped was because too many turds landed on his garage roof. I think he was starting to clue in.

Bulb

The prick who invented neckties must have been a masochist.

LFBF

If you chew dominantly on one side, does that make your teeth on the other side coattail riders?

In-Th
The grappa clock seems to work off a thirty-six-minute hour.

LFBF
Why do they make so many stuffed animals and other kid toys look so fucking creepy?

Bulb
Porter's, Barb's, and 3D's four-pound neutered dog still has more balls than Wilson's grandkid.

Gov't
Do all senior government jobs require applicants to have repeated grade seven a minimum of three times?

$$$$
Grappa is a kind of truth serum.

In-Th
I think I need some vitamin ZZZZZZ.

B.M.
The only accomplishment we do alone is deciding if we can or can't.

LFBF
Why do pomegranates make my shit smell like asparagus?

????
Walk before you run ... That's the politically correct 2.0 way of saying, "Shit your pants and crawl."

T.S.
I was once on stage with Eddie Van Halen as he soloed and contemplated grabbing his guitar and running, but I quickly realized I'd likely never walk again.

In-Th

I know three LeRoys, and they're all quiet and kind. I also know a guy named Lennox (after the boxer or singer I guess), and he's a fucking idiot … I got distracted watching *Sports Centre* highlights and forgot where I was going with this …

In-Th

"One more shot" = piss-poor spelling and questionable writing.

LFBF

Do airlines purposely try to make people go batshit nuts with small seats made from cactus and recycled asbestos, with shitty service, and Disney movies so they can charge an extra security tax?

$$$$

Find a couple of lists of scared-mommy clubs on the internet that list their membership and sell them blocks of stocks in Nerf and bubble wrap.

TFUW

"If history has taught us nothing …" it was likely taught by a politically correct crybaby.

Bulb

Steve Earl knew his math and his mash.

Bulb

Smoking a cigar while a self-righteous, it's all-about-me PITA (pain in the ass) passively acts like you're killing him as he waves his arms like he's swatting a swarm of mosquitoes and not giving a big creamy shit about him makes you look cooler.

LFBF

What the hell happened with all the criminals during the onset of the coronavirus? For fuck's sakes, we all have masks on! Missed opportunity for dumb fucks in a dick profession.

In-Th

Money is not how corrections are made.

B.M.

Time is the ultimate mind fuck.

LFBF

Why do words hurt only in First World counties?

Gov't

I once had political aspirations and even took steps toward them until one day I realized that instead of swilling coffee, free lunches, and getting a giant, unwarranted pension, I'd likely be doing twelve to fifteen for strangling one of the other career dipshits on the council.

????

If that creepy dude Vincent Price and that chick that banged Prince and Nikki Sixx ever had a love child, would it be a rock?

LFBF

As we are all destined for the dirt, the only question is, what do we do before that happens?

Bulb

Eighties music was 20 percent total dogshit, 35 percent great, and 45 percent What the fuck was that? Unlike now, when it's 99.4 percent computerized dick dribble.

Bulb

If you're the nose-wipe goody-goody who stops on a busy road to let someone else in causing everyone behind you to lock it up because you think of yourself as being a good Samaritan, you need to be kicked hard in the short and curlys.

In-Th

Sitting in a hot tub with a $90 bottle of booze and a $30 cigar is far better therapy than lying on a couch and pity-crying to some putz who gets paid to listen to you while he draws goat stick figures with big penises.

Bulb

A broken car heater in parts of Canada can literally be a death sentence in eight out of the twelve months ...

In-Th

At times, I drink maybe a little more than I should, and I've used the excuse that once something is open, it goes bad faster. For example, fruit—once pierced, it does go bad fast, and grappa is made with grape stuff, and if the bottle is now open ...

TFUW

Note to sci-fi nerds: the Jedi mind trick doesn't work. I've tried it so hard on more than one occasion that my head almost burst trying to get people to go home or get the hell out of my office when they have overstayed their welcomes, and nothing ...!

B.M.

The other shoe drops far less often when you keep both on your feet.

$$$$

Get the rights to the song "You Got Another Thing Coming" and license it to UPS or FedEx for the next decade or so.

Bulb

Everyone has incredible potential, but for far too many, then the diaper comes off and ...

Bulb
When the letters I write start resembling squiggly lines and every word is spelled phonetically, I know I'm drunk usually starting around six to nine shots and definitely by twelve (by which I mean when the twenty-six-ounce bottle I'm drinking from is down to twelve ounces or less).

Gov't
Politics 101: swill coffee, moisten a chair, piss away money that isn't yours, steal others' freedoms and rights by use of idealistic, improbable fear on the naive only to sell it back to them in the form of fees, licenses, and taxes and upon retirement or not being reelected collect unjust, inflated pensions for the all of the above.

In-Th
Nonino always kept me in control, both the man and the booze.

WTF
Waterproof bug spray? So how do you get that stinky shit off before going to bed? Or are you stuck funkying up the sheets and not getting laid until it wears off?

LFBF
Is IKEA Swedish for "Ha ha! The directions that come with our particle board shit came from a Mr. Potato Head coloring book"?

Bulb
The maître d' at one of our favorite restaurant often gives me a shot of grappa when we sit down with the excuse "Bam, help me out. Someone, she order it but no want it now. Can I offer it to you?" I think he thinks I'm mobbed up.

T.S.
Flavored soap isn't flavored; it's scented and apparently tastes like a shitty tea. (I gave my buddy $5 to try it).

$$$$

Women have Lululemon for pants, so invent "Stuffed Baked Potato" pants for men.

LFBF

Is kale the tipping point for mankind's starting to eat weeds and insects?

Gov't

Snot-nosed, spoiled, trust-fund kids without any blue-collar experience make the shittiest politicians.

Bulb

Coping and grieving are both solo journeys.

In-Th

I have created monsters and millionaires, and on at least one occasion, one of my creations was both.

Bulb

Everyone has opinions, but if they don't have a possible answer or remedy tied to them that can justify the thought, they are worth the value of nut sweat. Justin, I'm looking at you ...

T.S.

I cry silently deep inside every time I hear an original anything that has been altered and/or sanitized to play on network TV or on the radio.

Bulb

"There is strength in numbers"? The only strength in numbers is in bank accounts or in the size of O linemen. There's sheeple mentality in a mass number of people. Real strength comes only from within.

LFBF

Why hasn't crime spiked now that everyone everywhere is masked up, or has media found something else to simonize?

B.M.

Never rush it. Words that relate to everything.

LFBF

With everyone hoarding toilet paper for the second time in 2020, I have to assume there's going to be a lot more "accidental" drunk smoking cigarettes house fires. Is this the start of the backslide that takes us all into the early days of a *Walking Dead* and *Mad Max* society?

Bulb

Survival of the fittest will be the downfall of today's everyone is equal youth.

T.S.

The scene in *Casino* where Pesci says, "A hundred bucks to whoever hits the plane." We've done this on more than one occasion and with several other forms of transportation.

Bulb

Nope, even large amounts of alcohol can't make Trevor Noah interesting. The only thing that does is changing the channel.

WTF

You know 2020 was a fucked-up year when Air Canada (which has all but been grounded during this and voted consistently as one of the worst airlines in the world) is making money for their investors. Huh?

Bulb

Some wars will never end.

LFBF
Weight Watchers has Oprah as its spokesperson? Huh? 'Nuff said.

Bulb
All lakes have skeletons in them.

In-Th
Call it a moderate degree of paranoia, but I have seen firsthand how shitty mankind deals with life during times of uncertainty and stress. Interestingly enough, people living in the Third World don't fare nearly as poorly or fall as far as we, the privileged in the alleged First World, do.

LFBF
Do wild horses exist anymore? The animals or the people?

Bulb
I owe an apology to a guy who cut me and three others off today. I thought he was such a shitty driver that he must have worked for Uber. I was wrong. When I caught up to him at the next set of lights, I saw the Skip the Dishes sticker. A distinction with little difference, but I own my mistakes …

B.M.
Irony of life: We fight and work our asses off every minute of our lives for a little piece of dirt to call our own to which we will all eventually return to and be covered with.

TFUW
The guy wearing horns and a diaper who took part in the invasion of the Capitol building was on a hunger strike after being arrested because the jailers wouldn't give him organic carrots and free-range apples. How did they put an end to it? The prison gave in … I don't have the words for how much stupidity was involved here. I have

never been more content and committed to just doing my thing, not interfering with anyone else's shit, and just watching the world burn in my rearview mirror while silently sipping a grappa and saying to myself, *Yup, I'm good, just toss another log on …*

In-Th

Anyone whose baggage is only a carry-on or a backpack is likely to be an incredibly dull dinner guest.

Bulb

Smartphones are nothing more than electronic leashes.

In-Th

It might be time to go to bed as I'm somehow guessing that my wife isn't going to like the fact that it would appear I just bought both the *Bugs Bunny* and *Scooby Doo* complete box sets.

List 4
Things That Don't Exist Any Longer or Won't Very Soon

↪ **Fax Machines.** Except in my office and about a dozen of the major businesses I deal with regularly as they still believe this dinosaur technology is a secure form of communication.

↪ **Records.** Also 8-tracks, cassettes, CDs, and decent new music.

↪ **Froshing.** A once semi-harmless rite of passage for initiating new students that likely died on the vine when some snot-nosed kid's mommy went to bitch-slap the principal verbally when her little Johnny came home covered in shaving cream and eggs.

↪ **Credible Politicians.** Sorry. This one is kind of urban legend that since I wrote it down, I have been having a hard time finding evidence that they ever existed.

↪ **Sears Catalogues.** Before the internet, getting a catalogue in the mail and picking out the crap you wanted Santa to bring you in hopes your folks told your grandparents before grandma could knit you another ugly sweater with a duck on it or wrap up a pair of argyle socks for you was huge.

↪ **Spankings.** Back in the day, when a kid did something stupid and got caught, kids got their asses paddled by parents as a lesson to either not do it again or get better at it. To this day, I still have wooden spoons splinters in my ass cheeks courtesy of my mom, and I deserved most of them.

↪ **Travelers Checks**. Very possibly the stupidest financial vehicle ever thought up but strangely vastly popular (until someone actually tried to use them). They were bank checks people could take on vacation rather than carrying cash so in the event they were robbed abroad, the value could be claimed before criminals could take advantage of them. Problem was that outside major North American cities, no shopkeeper wanted them as a form of payment; thus, they became very expensive toilet paper until you got back home and cashed them in minus the bank service charges.

- **Thick Skin.** 'Nuff said. Words hurt only when we let them.
- **Visionaries.** Days gone by, man created flight, automobiles, radio, television, the internet, microwave popcorn, indoor plumbing, popsicles, hair plugs ... Today, everyone is so consumed with everyone else's business or creating a million-dollar app that nothing revolutionary is being dreamed up. Even the Jetsons thought we'd have flying cars by now. Musk, you're the exception.
- **Classic Cars.** Cars were once works of art. They had style, sleek looks that made heads turn, and earth-shaking sounds. They have now been replaced with cookie-cutter, mass-produced, disposable *meh* that are about as interesting as bowling balls. I feel fairly safe in assuming that no future car collectors will have a classic Nissan, Kia, Prius, or Volvo in their collections.
- **Heroes.** Every kid once had a hero whether it was John Wayne, Walter Payton, Wonder Woman, or even old dad, and they all swore by them. But with all the distractions our world now has, today's heroes have life spans that if they last until the end of the movie, they're doing well.
- **PC-Free Media.**-TV shows such as *Seinfeld* made over $4 billion with episodes about nothing. No messages, no life lessons ... Just their simple versions of comedy. Now, everything you watch or listen to comes with a message of a fight for whatever rights or justice or the way everyone needs to be. Even sporting events are now guilty of this.
- **Kitchen Phones.** No kid today will ever know the embarrassment of a boy calling a girl for the first time and her dear old dad answering the phone. Nor will anyone running to the bathroom during commercials be clotheslined by his or her kid pulling the phone cord as taut as possible into his or her bedroom to hide behind the door for some perceived privacy. No young man will ever know the hell of calling a girl he likes for the first time only to end up making small talk with her mother for half an hour before she hands the phone to her daughter. Innocent embarrassment-built character, and that no longer exists.

→ **Real Lawn Darts.** Because in today's overprotective world in which inanimate objects are blamed rather than who's actually at fault for accidents, kids are so stupid that lawn darts in their hands are seen as a stone's throw away from becoming the chosen weapon used by mass murders and the very dangerous. FYI, anything in the hands of someone not familiar with it or taught how to use it is dangerous. Someone throws a rock that takes out another's eye, the rock's at fault?

→ **Public Libraries.** Except for being restrooms for the homeless, places for stay-at-home mommies to dump their kids off for an hour puppet show, and places for municipalities to show they really don't know what the hell they're doing with tax dollars, libraries are now totally useless. Between online, downloading, and minimal reading done nowadays, these places are on the endangered species list somewhere near common sense, good manners, and black rhinos.

→ **Smoking Sections.** This one I'm actually okay with. I never really understood how half a restaurant or theater was designated smoking and the other half non. Airplanes and buses were even stupider. They're giant, sealed, metal, toilet paper tubes! Where the fuck did they think the smoke was going to go?

→ **Old-Time Hockey.** Really, the way football, hockey, and other contact sports were played with full intensity and fire burning in everyone's belly—modern-day gladiator sports. They were violent. The players were warriors going to battle for fame, fortune, and glory. They knew what they were getting into. Chances were that if you played, you were going to get bloody. Getting hurt was a risk most were willing to take rather than working at their uncle's lumberyard driving a skidsteer for the next thirty years. Now, the heart is more in the contract than in the game. Hockey fights now look more like two guys in an all-boys' school learning to dance, and the game has started to look more like the Ice Capades. If football keeps going in the same direction, guys will eventually be yelling, "Red rover, red rover, we call Joey over!" rather than tackling.

EIGHT SHOTS

Bulb
Three options in life:

    A) being a working-class dog,
    B) a fat cat, or
    C) a fucking parasite.

Bulb
Mick got it. Childhood living is easy to do.

TFUW
In today's world, could I get away with saying, "I'm not drunk. I'm grappa infused"?

WTF
I miss the eighties. I remember a kid bringing a bag of frozen brussels sprouts to school for lunch. Today, those parents would have been taken away and on the evening news.

B.M.
No one should ever live off money made from someone else's sweat who didn't earn it first.

In-Th

I think Henry brushes his teeth with an imaginary toothbrush.

LFBF

How much of a privileged vagina was the guy who came up with the smart car?

T.S.

Finding inspiration for this book was never what I would call "hard work."

LFBF

If a humanitarian goes to a war zone to preach his or her personal beliefs about God or war or grape nuts cereal or whatever and gets detained, can that be considered a crime against the mentally challenged?

Bulb

There's a good reason Football Sunday starts in the afternoon. The NFL gods truly knew their target market.

$$$$

If soap was mandatory, we could put many taxi companies and Uber out of business.

In-Th

Mikey Myers and Freddy both wouldn't have made it in our neighborhood growing up.

TFUW

No one's dead grandfather would ever have believed the word *warrior* has now been replaced with *political activist*.

Bulb

Shitty people are and will always be shitty people; it's just that some of them know how to smile when they're being shitty and convince the masses they aren't as shitty as others know them to be. Many of them become used-car salesmen, TV writers, politicians, and airline customer-service reps.

Bulb
Bourbon is the little brother of grappa, but they both came from the same tough-guy family.

B.M.
Make every move count.

T.S.
I once cheated in a jalapeño-eating contest and lost on purpose so I could watch the other poor bastard painfully claim victory and sweat all over his crappy $8 trophy and ribbon that he actually wiped his nose on.

LFBF
When did tough guys stop wearing suits?

Bulb
Jimmy's hair looks like he was run over by a combine.

LFBF
Dumb-fuck kids who eat Tide Pods ... Shouldn't we be encouraging them to share some with their parents?

T.S.
At some lame patio party I was once at, they went around the fire pit and everyone had to say what was the stupidest thing he or she had ever done while drinking. The answers were shit like "doing Jell-O shots" or "going to class drunk." I got up and left when it was my turn. I didn't have the heart to say it was attending that nerd party.

TFUW
Never more than now has yesterday's world been more interesting, and the coronavirus had little to do with it.

Bulb
Listening to dumb shit can help with thought expression and creativity but *not* with anger issues.

Gov't
Don't play the Trudeau drinking game while drinking anything stronger than diet Coke. Anything else in the quantities you're about to consume is deadly dangerous.

LFBF
Did Scooby Doo ever tell Shaggy he needed a shower?

$$$$
If I could turn my male bulldog's crap into gold, he truly would be my golden goose.

Bulb
A male wearing red or green pants may be silently crying out for help.

LFBF
Why the fuck didn't some guy living in the desert invent Kleenex?

TFUW
In a relatively high-end restaurant in a resort town, I asked the twenty-year-old bubblehead maître d' where I could get coffee and do some paperwork while my wife got a massage, and her reply was, "Well … Uhh, I think there's a Chili's two blocks down … Oh, and there's also a gas station down that way." Today's world is fucking doomed.

Bulb

Jägermeister is the K-pop of booze as both make anyone with any taste sick and full of regret.

In-Th

Can a pen's ink be traced back to who put it there?

LFBF

If you go on a merry-go-round and not throw up, what was the point?

TFUW

Fucking CDC gave out a warning about people drinking hand sanitizer after a couple died and a few others went blind. Did you dipshits learn nothing from Darwin? STFU!

In-Th

Where has all the time gone? Only last week, I was, like, sixteen. "A blink and it's over" is one of the truest statements ever made.

B.M.

A trip anywhere becomes a hard fall for anyone not paying attention.

T.S.

When life hands Ronnie lemons, he tosses them into a bucket, dumps them out into the mud, shits in the bucket, picks up the dirty fruit, wipes his ass with them, hangs the soiled fruit from his rearview mirror, and wears the bucket home as a rain hat. Nope, no lemonade for that guy …

LFBF

Why don't nerds overthrow the world?

????

Gas station beef jerky is the tractor pull of meat products.

In-Th

The chunk of hard shit I just blew from my nose was the size of a marble. Maybe I had a tumor?

LFBF

Mint is considered to be the sense of happy and freshness just as garlic is considered to stink, but which one is used more in cooking? And haven't we all been told time and again to use all our senses when eating a great meal? Who decides this shit?

WTF

Coal placed under pressure will eventually turn into a diamond, but corn in the poop chute still has the strength to maintain its form. Huh?

LFBF

How hungry was the first poor bastard who said, "Let's eat the snot from an oyster"?

T.S.

My computer guy (whatever his name is) takes a lot of shit from me. He's decent at what he does, but he's also a lazy dork.

LFBF

Does voting socialist in a capitalist society make you an anarchist, shit disturber, or someone who should be wearing a helmet and snorkel in the shower?

Bulb

I think Jim's patio light was once used on the stage of *Star Search*.

In-Th

They say the good die young. Reggie, Adamo, and Frank, you're all proof of that. I'll likely make it to five-plus centuries if that's the case.

Gov't

An active river flows to an ocean and feeds the world, but an active politician only empties the world's pockets to feed no one but himself.

LFBF

If I took an accidental emergency piss in a laundry basket, could I get away with it by saying that they needed a different detergent?

In-Th

Some of the most popular male names in the world are Lucas, Noah, Caleb, Muhammad, and Grayson, but I can think of only four people with them, yet I know over fifty named either Wilbur, Eugene, Melvin, Lloyd, Leonard, or Alfred. Huh?

Bulb

Never drink from the green bottle at Rich's place in the mountains.

T.S.

I put a frozen dog turd under the grill of a guy's barbecue at a house I was showing when I was selling real estate because he'd been a dick to my client and his wife.

????

PC warriors are nothing more than the furniture polish of humans.

WTF

What the hell does GCB feed his kids, crystal meth? And when the fuck do they go to bed?

In-Th

I need to get someone in the immediate neighborhood to become one of those couponing hoarders so when the zombies or liberals or covid 3.0 hits and everyone goes into mass paranoia looting 7-11s and Wal-Mart's, I can use his or her place to do my shopping. Maybe

I'll start dropping hints to that young couple or that prick with the rental stuff to start doing it …

B.M.
People who live their lives in chains should strive to become master lock picks rather than fighting to break them.

LFBF
Is becoming the best at something that isn't worth doing worth the effort?

Bulb
If you have never seen the bottom, you'll likely have a hard time recognizing the top.

TFUW
Flipping channels, I saw there was some sort of one of those inspiring documentaries showing successful women—Kim Kardashian, Paris Hilton, and Britney Spears. Great choices for inspirational success stories—a twat shot, a twat shot with a rich grandfather, and a sweet, innocent child performer who went batshit, fall-on-the-floor, speaking-in-tongues crazy as an adult with a bonus twat shot. Great fucking role models for young girls.

B.M.
Shoot for the stars … How about aiming at getting out of debt and not being someone's burden?

T.S.
I made $10k at a funeral for six maybe eight sentences.

$$$$
Our snot-nosed, slow-witted, "Mommy, cut my meat," Richie Rich, trust fund PM just pledged something like $250 million to black

business owners to help them. Isn't that textbook racism? The guy is too dense to realize that banks don't decide yay or nay based on the color of your skin because for them, all debtors regardless of color, sex, or personal orientation are pure profit.

He's also the blank-stare, two rocks rolling around in an empty can moron who had a personal black-faced scandal roughly a year earlier. The money maker idea—pick up stock in Ancestry.com or find a kid who can print fake birth certificates because everyone in Canada is about to become about .5-3 percent black.

In-Th
I just head-butted my pear tree trying to take a piss through the fence. I think I'm bleeding ...

In-Th
Goofball haircuts are a direct 218% result of drugs, dense parents, and a societal resentment.

Bulb
Note to anyone starting out: Good manners are an asset but nothing compared to the ability to do what you were hired for and to follow through. Lack of either means getting used to ugly uniforms, name tags, and asking customers if they want fries with that.

????
Unicorns—mythical white horses with wings and petrified penises on their foreheads and considered signs of a rare utopia, but I doubt the guy standing under one flying overhead and getting a creamy, steaming horse turd dropped on him sees them that way.

LFBF
In today's world, would the idea of Michael Jackson becoming white be a hate crime?

Bulb

Wheaties should be eaten only by cows and horses.

TFUW

My grandma used to take her old plastic pill bottles and chunks of crayons and melt them down in the stove to make goofy shit for us grandkids. No thoughts or worries about fumes or chem trails or any other nasty stuff coming off it as it melted, but in today's world, a straw being used in public and an ice cube tray are considered the downfall of mankind. Huh? Maybe we need to just find simple shit that makes us happy again.

LFBF

Adam and Eve committed the original sin by eating an apple from the Tree of the Knowledge of Good and Evil. What weren't they supposed to find out? And if they were the origin of mankind and told to go forth and multiply, doesn't that make us all the result of incest? And if dust is 80 percent dead skin, how the fuck did God make the first dude, Adam, and from it?

B.M.

Only a retard thinks working with retards has anything to do with anyone mentally challenged.

In-Th

Internet warriors need their asses kicked.

WTF

Goat yoga? What the hell is wrong with some people? What sheep molester came up with this cherry of an idea?

T.S.

In the 1990s, Bobby DeNiro and I both made livings by driving buses made thirty or forty years earlier.

Bulb

Life is very much like people on the highway. They go off in every direction, and some people find exotic, beautiful, less-traveled ones, some drive like hell, crash, burn, and die before they even figured out where they were going, but the bulk just blindly get stuck behind countless others only to get frustrated, give everyone the finger, race into the fast lane, and then do fifteen km/h slower than the speed limit screaming into the mirror with their blinkers on and only clue in to how stupid they looked as they are about to exit either the highway or life itself.

LFBF

Is there a correlation between women getting yeast infections and the amount of wine they spill?

In-Th

When I grow up, I want to either be Sonny Crockett or a weatherman.

Bulb

Every generation thinks they are the chosen ones who grew up in a utopian time and don't realize until many years after their youth is long behind them that the generation just prior to theirs actually had it better.

LFBF

Can anyone on that *Storage Wars* show even spell *storage*?

In-Th

Maintaining is harder than accelerating or slowing down.

$$$$

10 + 10 x 10 = 2 1/2 in 1.

Gov't
Real fireworks that explode and actually kill thousands are made during political debates by blowhard stuffed shirts with puffed-out chests and coiffed hair, not in Chinese warehouses.

Bulb
Both of the guys who got there before and after you also think the "home" they found are only theirs also.

B.M.
Growing old happens only for the lucky, the strategists, and more often than not, the overly timid who never actually lived a life before they got there.

Bulb
Fluffy shit in the end is just fluffy shit without substance, and it flushes fast.

In-Th
I need someone to teach me how to fly a helicopter ...

LFBF
Do the *Real Housewives of ...* wherever realize that the real world (not the stupid fucking MTV show) see them as real stupid and real spoiled, whiny, pains in the asses?

Bulb
Being what others would consider damaged doesn't mean we can't function without help; it just means you need to find another way other than the one convention has taught us was the only way.

Bulb
Fakers, posers, and wannabes are time-wasting, human grass stains. Be yourself, not some other dipshit.

B.M.
We live so soft in North America, yet far too few have experienced anything else to even understand this. .

LFBF
Do street dealers who sell anything and everything to the same people over and over see themselves as pharmacists without licenses, and if so, do pharmacists who chronically refill pain meds to the same people ever feel like drug dealers?

T.S.
I have had epiphanies at one, four, seven, midnight, and every hour in between. The point I'm making is open your mind; your heart and self and inspiration will always find you.

In-Th
Navigating Christmas decor and crap is a hell of a lot harder than one might think after number eight.

$$$$
I'm not much of a bacon fan, but I realize a huge number of people would eat a phonebook sandwich if it had bacon in it or a bacon-covered diaper given the chance. Create an all-bacon restaurant and call it "The Heart Attack Grill."

LFBF
Where can I get an actual fire fighter's hose? Because I got some pretty disturbing shit pop up on the internet when I typed in something like "fireman-sized hose."

In-Th
Both the ficus and lemon tree died because of me ... But I still tell people it was suicide by both of them.

Gov't

Why do we name airports, streets, and parks after forgettable political opportunists instead of people who have actually made real impacts on mankind such as the inventor of pizza or pro wrestlers?

TFUW

Why the fuck are shitty TV channels allowed to alter movies and TV shows to make them PG-13 friendly? Isn't that the same as wiping boogers on someone else's artwork in a museum?

B.M.

Room to run can't happen with a leash and choke collar on.

T.S.

"Crab apples taste like shit and are the perfect throwing size, like a golf ball, so it's only natural what to do with them. When God speaks, I listen …" That's what I told the cop when I got caught as a kid doing just that, and it worked. He didn't call me parents.

Bulb

"One-Eyed Wally" has a good eye.

????

Shitting the bed happens only after you go all in and put a full effort into anything. Failure comes from anything less than that.

Bulb

I'm willing to bet God is not a fan of the NFL.

B.M.

The only way to "see it coming" is if you have your eyes open.

In-Th

This book is either going to sell like 10¢ beer or embarrass and mortify the shit out of me.

LFBF
How long before professional sports become the next casualty of political correctness and start enforcing everyone-must-play policies and handing out participation trophies?

B.M.
Savor the flavors of life while you can as you won't likely get them again. There are no second helpings in life.

Bulb
A rocking chair is a sad replacement for a driver's license.

In-Th
A watched pizza never comes.

T.S.
I, like many, knife fight my inner voices every day and night to do the right things instead of the easy things. That is what makes the world a better place and is the difference between winners, those who settle, and flat-out losers.

Bulb
I knew we might be living privileged lives when we ran in to Barb and 3D at Costco and Barb said they were buying a fancy toilet brush for when guests came over. I'm pretty sure she was joking, but I started thinking, *Do we need to buy one for this also?*

In-Th
Damn, I think a neighbor just caught me chucking jujubes at the kids screwing around in our back lane.

LFBF
Do indoor plants ever kick back on a leaf looking outside and think, *Damn. We got it pretty good. Look at those poor bastards outside freezing covered in dog piss and bird shit and never getting to watch HBO.*

List 5
Things as Pathetic and/or as Useless as a Gun with No Bullets

Decaf espresso

Doing a marathon in sweat socks

AM only radios

A kale salad

Rap music

G-strings on fat people

Smelling salts in coroner kits for dead guys

Zero-alcohol beer

Guys named Justin

Empty toilet paper rolls

Kindergarten scissors

Airline customer service

Any vegan restaurant

Sixties movies

Social media keyboard warriors

Mario's brother Luigi

Top hats on guys with topknots

Topknots

CBC Canada

The Oprah Network

B-day gift cards after age eighty

Greta the whiner

Actual new books written for teens

Wide-screen TVs

Bowling

Open-faced ski masks

Shot glasses after 3:00 a.m.

YouTube's six-second ads

Statues of forgettable political leaders

Vita water

Sugar-free desserts

Single ply ass wipes

Gun laws to stop criminals

Vegas weddings

The TLC network

High-end condos in shitty neighborhoods

Christian gangsta rap

Christian rock

All gangsta rap

People who use words like *gangsta*

Christmas in June sales crap

St. Valentine's Day

Low-calorie pizza

Vegan hamburgers

Airfare "sales"

Bigfoot

Canadian Senate

Diet food

Time-outs in school

Watching video gamers

Parsley as a garnish

Jails to reform criminals

Cable TV

No-failing grades in schools

Participation trophies

Clocks in hospital waiting areas

Diet water (Look it up. It's real.)

Described video so the blind can *watch* and enjoy TV

Saving the planet from invasive plastic straws

A chain smoker's toothbrush

Dollar-store condoms

NINE SHOTS

B.M.
The sweet spot is always out of reach for someone farsighted.

LFBF
Based on above, are nearsighted people incapable of planning or seeing anything far off?

Bulb
Kids who draw on walls and furniture have creative impulses their parents often miss and punish; thus, I encourage them when I go to other people's houses. I like to help.

In-Th
I think if reincarnation is real, I want to come back as one of those little kamikaze birds too small to be hunted and just fly around shitting on whatever catches their eye and stealing kids' lunches before I head south to ride out winter.

T.S.
I once named a dog "Crotch Licker" for no particular reason, and my uncle Jackie had one we all called "Wiener" because every time you tried to get out of a car on his farm, the dog would run over and jam his head into your wiener.

LFBF

Pigs spend their lives in mud and shit, so what starving hillbilly said, "Hey! Let's pickle their feet and eat them"?

TFUW

My grandfather and great-grandfather never would have dodged bullets only to allow this generation to dodge work.

Bulb

In the light of the next day, the night before usually seems darker than it was.

LFBF

If making ends meet means struggling hard enough to barely cover your costs, does years apart mean "Fuck it! Who gives a shit?"

In-Th

Starbucks, you have been slipping for the last couple of years.

Bulb

My little guy would have been a great wingman.

Bulb

A waterbed that leaked was once a sign of virility.

T.S.

The grandfatherly advice I got as a kid went something like this: "Find a woman pleasing to your ear as well as your eye because eventually you'll both likely be fat with hair in all the wrong places, and if you don't, then you'll be two ugly people with nothing to say to each other."

????

If a cat rules a house, is that the result of a dog acting too passive?

WTF
My male bulldog has turned into a couch licker. What the fuck is this thing made of?

Gov't
If the coronavirus can be killed off with Lysol, why aren't world leaders expropriating it and spraying that shit on everything? The world could be saved and smell lemony fresh, and it would maybe be the first time someone flying Air Canada wouldn't have a sticky tray table. (Written March 28, 2020.)

LFBF
How the hell do some people with advanced degrees seemingly get stupider after going to university?

Bulb
8-6-2-4-3-5-0 = 28, the same age Bon Scott was when the song was first written … I think.

In-Th
I think the last fart may have fooled me …

TFUW
Working without a net needs to happen far more often nowadays.

Bulb
"Moth to a flame" is a semi-polite way of describing abject stupidity.

LFBF
How the hell is the guy who invented internet porn not the richest dude in world and able to buy the fucking solar system?

Bulb
Lemmy got it.

In-Th

Had my parents over for a $100 prime rib roast and pasta with a homemade sauce that took the better part of a day to slow cook. The roast was so tender and tasty that Tony Bourdain and Gordon Ramsey would have been drooling into their white chefs' jackets when my pops said, "Ahh, everything tastes like shit to me now." Normally, I wait until after dinner to have a couple of shots, but tonight, I started early …

T.S.

A colleague who used to drive me nuts with his insufferable whining went on holiday, so I filled his desk with all his files and shit inside full of $150 worth of rice.

Bulb

The Easter Bunny could kick the shit out of the Tooth Fairy, and Santa wouldn't be anything without his gnome winter army and attack deer.

WTF

Vance is such a retard that he has sent a text to my landline on more than one occasion only to hang up and then text the same message to the same number again within thirty seconds thinking he sent one to my cell and the other to the moon I guess …

LFBF

Is the fear of hell less scary since the invention of Zippo lighters?

Bulb

One Direction, huge in 2010: "Do you want paper or plastic?" In 2015: "Did you bring your own bag or want one of ours for five cents?" In 2020: "This is my park bench. You can't make me leave! I was once in something called One Direction in 2030."

????

The second bottle of anything weighs more and cost a shitload more long term than the first every time, and the only cure is bananas and strawberries with sprinkles, but don't use them to write with.

Bulb

Cats are shady fucks. One just swiped my bulldog across the nose for no reason as they were just enjoying each other's stink.

LFBF

If everyone was taught to play a musical instrument instead of what to think, would we have less crying and more Waylon?

TFUW

Days gone by, people wanted to solve the mysteries of mankind (yes, Justin, it's pronounced mankind, not peoplekind, you twit). People wanted to find Bigfoot, kids wanted to see Santa, figure out how they built the pyramids, see if there was life on Mars, wonder who actually ate those gross chocolate Easter eggs with the sweet goop in them, etc. In today's fucked-up world, the only answers kids want are about Instagram shit.

T.S.

My beautiful wife and I gave ourselves accidental colon cleanses the night before Fishbelly's birthday.

????

The remote is a black peanut with fingers and numbers.

B.M.

Jack Daniels should get both the Nobel Peace Prize and be charged with war crimes.

WTF

How the fuck is this a book? I have 500-plus thoughts, ideas, epiphanies, and allegories; 200 make sense, 200 are accurate, and about 150 are written in what I have to assume is Aramaic. Fuck it. Where's my shot glass at?

In-Th

Technology and I have never been friends, but for the love of God and peanut butter, eighty-five-year-old George had to teach me how to use the remote for my cable box. Maybe I should take a class in some of this shit.

LFBF

Rick Ashley? How the fuck did his crap pop up in my videos? Drink and anchor, you dork.

B.M.

Stupidity is an art we need to stop funding.

Bulb

Mr. Roarke sold Tattoo short.

$$$$

JT could make up for all his spending by dressing like a clown and letting people squirt water into his mouth like they do at carnivals with the exploding balloons.

LFBF

Do they make toilet freshener smell like summer rain to make you go more often?

In-Th

As the world tries to give each other a hand job to make it a better place, does that finally make me special for not playing into this shit?

LFBF
Do any ethical dentists actually give out sugar-free candies at Halloween, or do they use the night to build their businesses?

Bulb
In the eighties, vaping would have been the smelly vagina of smoking.

LFBF
Hollywood is allegedly a third gay, and a derogatory term for gay was once *fruit*. If the other two-thirds are made up of money-hungry wackos, is that where the old saying "The only things you find in Hollywood are fruits and nuts" comes from?

Bulb
I remember being told once that thunder was only God cleaning his house. Come on. Even a dumb-fuck kid knows he'd have people for that.

B.M.
Spelling is a sober man's game; fucking spellcheck is a drunk's menace.

In-Th
More of the eighties and nineties sucked than didn't, but not to the level of the 80 to 90 percent that does now.

$$$$
Make prisoners do an interview with most any rapper. Sell idea to the government as a hard form of interrogation instead of waterboarding.

LFBF
If God is religious, whom does he pray to? I'm betting Buddha.

Bulb
Darts, curling, and rhythmic gymnastics are the bowling of the nonball sports.

In-Th

Pens could someday soon end up doing jail time.

LFBF

Did radical alarmists see the White House as offensive when Obama was running the show?

TFUW

I don't know anyone who plays video games and only just discovered some chair moisteners that do actually have fans that watch them play and follow them, and these dorks can even get paid for it ... What the fuck happened to us?

T.S.

If you wake up in a field, in a canoe, or wrapped in a tablecloth, it means you likely really got fucked up the night before. Trust me. Voice of experience.

LFBF

Is drinking too much beer and getting fat God's way of saying, "Get off your lazy ass and get a better job so you can afford the good stuff"?

In-Th

Fuck. I just found another big black mole! Next day—hindsight. Several grappas and a black marker with no cap don't mix and can induce paranoia and panic.

Bulb

My pool table has a lot of balls ...

????

A thousand to one; a $1,000 buy-in is still a smarter investment than a thirty-year Radio Shack career.

In-Th
I should have died eighteen times already … Drunk math.

Bulb
The guy who came up with the elves making cookies in trees ad campaign likely smoked a lot of leaves first.

T.S.
I have never sold out.

$$$$
Booze-flavored popsicles. Adults would gobble them up on hot summer days, and kids would all try to sneak them.

LFBF
I wonder if Jimmy Buffett ever got fucked up with a dolphin?

Bulb
Being a country singer is one of the only ways a backwoods hillbilly with shitty teeth can gets babes to fuck him.

B.M.
Fate may have the final say about where we all end up, but we get to decide which direction we take and how fast we get there.

TFUW
In today's world, yesterday's successes are tomorrow's demons.

$$$$
Cheesy squeeze …

T.S.
I'm a suit and tie–wearing, ethnic, country boy eighties head banger with all my teeth and hair.

Bulb

The acronym for success is EDDSS

> Effort
> Desire
> Drive
> Stamina
> See beyond all the shit

Bulb

Every aspect of life is about marketing and product awareness.

TFUW

A bird in the hand is worth two in the bush. That means nothing if you don't know how to cook it and refuse to learn.

Bulb

Someday soon, lifestyle will be nothing more than a Google program or a cell phone app.

In-Th

My freezer contents are worth more than Rusty.

????

It took three.

Bulb

I was half-assed watching that *Bar Rescue* show and the loudmouth guy was teaching the bar people in some backwater hill town how to make complex drinks and food that would make their toothless patrons happy. I'm guessing that could have been as simple as moonshine mouthwash and applesauce.

In-Th

My beautiful wife parks like someone is chasing her.

LFBF

Is there a secret competition between the fast-food places to see which one can kill off more of their customers the fastest?

B.M.

Eat it, drink it, and read it, but first and foremost, learn from it.

Bulb

Some people have perfected the art of being shitty and unfortunately are often more than willing to display that and teach others how to duplicate it.

LFBF

Pockets are nothing more than bags sown into clothes. So does that make people who walk around with habitually full pockets internal bag ladies?

In-Th

The Russian ambassador who lived down the street from us was a spooky chick.

Bulb

The world after the coronavirus will have countless opportunities that only a few will act on. For the rest, it's going to be a hard, new bitch world.

B.M.

Everyone takes some licks and punches in the beginning of anything. Some endure, some don't. That's the difference between cutting your teeth and being able to eat steak or a life lived on cream of wheat and pablum.

In-Th

Number ten and several of his friends will be joining me tonight.

????

Spring folks often shit in cornflakes and work only when playing cards.

Bulb

Musicians are probably the best and the worst at surrounding themselves with the right people.

$$$$

Grappa Thoughts—fortune cookies.

In-Th

I'd like to run outside and make a snow angel, but my yard is covered in skunk, coyote, and squirrel shit …

LFBF

Where do all these modern keyboard warriors get all their pseudo strength from? Days gone by, the computer nerds and the typing class geeks used to get locked in their lockers until they had panic attacks and wet shorts, and the janitor had to let them out.

TFUW

If you're sleeping with the enemy, you understand they are the enemy and you made a conscious choice.

LFBF

Who the fuck invented a round pizza that he cut into triangles and later some genius figured it needed to go into a square box?

Gov't

Even though I'm truly politically agnostic, I did lose respect for the Democrats in the States when they were waiting for the ballot recount from Georgia and they didn't use that old Charlie Daniels song about Trump: "The devil went down to Georgia and he was lookin' for a soul to steal. He was in a bind and way behind and lookin' to make a deal." Opportunity missed.

In-Th
Fishbelly's and Marilyn's backyard is covered in marshmallows. Side note: my male bulldog loves misfires from my marshmallow gun.

B.M.
It's only overkill to those who oppose it.

T.S.
My grandfathers taught me opposite lessons, but they were both about survival and perseverance.

Bulb
When short pouring seems humane, it's time to pack up and go the fuck home.

????
Smart as a duck, strong as a bull, observant as a goat all make bad soup …

Bulb
Speeding up is always easier than slowing down in every way.

LFBF
Talk about a mental breakdown by a physically and mentally challenged guy. Where were the Frankenstein's Life Matters people when the town jumped the gun and burned him alive?

Bulb
From age sixteen to eighteen, I drove a huge, gas-guzzling, squirrel-poisoning, black smog–admitting truck and rarely ever paid for gas for it. Thanks, Jimbo.

B.M.

Life is simple. Aim and work for the sweet, high, cherry-red fruit and leave the low- hanging yellow ones alone unless you must and only to keep yourself going. The brown ones lying on the ground are road apples; don't touch them 'cause you're just going to get sick and end up with hands full of funk.

In-Th

I and people like me may be dinosaurs as our old world of common sense is dying, but unlike the actual dinosaurs, many of us DO see this giant meteor coming.

Bulb

Your real character will be immediately evident and come out the first time someone points a gun at you.

TFUW

We now give out participation awards for showing up to even the shittiest athletes, contestants, and competitors so they can display with pride something they didn't do jack shit to earn. Ya, that won't have any negative future impact on human behavior, will it?

Bulb

Mental, physical, and emotional exhaustion are all signs that you put in a full effort.

LFBF

If you work graveyard shifts and sleep during the day, are daydreams still considered a waste of time?

Bulb

No legend ever started from a couch except maybe during conception.

In-Th

Fucking hiccups ...

$$$$
Create the Kool-Aid Network channel for stupid people who believe dumb shit, and get Kim K and one of those greasy Jersey Shore jerk-offs to host it.

LFBF
Are liberals offended by Elmer Fudd and his gun?

B.M.
Always trust more than only what you see. (My bulldogs taught me that.)

Bulb
YouTube is brilliant at understanding drunk rhythm and feasting/exploiting the shit out of it.

In-Th
Fuck. I hope the garbage guy doesn't go through my trash. (Thank God it's not Russell anymore.)

LFBF
Who the fuck are we protecting by censoring language and criminals' faces on the evening news?

In-Th
It might be time I go to bed ... A dog was howling on TV, and my male bulldog perked up listening to it, so I just asked him to translate it for me.

B.M.
The person who finds a way to bottle ambition will become unspeakably rich and become one of the most hated people in history.

In-Th
Next year, just look at giving everyone a jar of frankincense for Christmas, but first find out what exactly frankincense is. I think it's a weed or something ...

List 6
Great Lines I Like from Movies, Music, Books, and Other Semi-Famous Crap

Twenty years for nothing. Well, that's nothing new. Besides, no one's interested in something you didn't do.

If you're going through hell, keep going.

Ring 3624–350. I lead a life of crime.

I'll give you something big enough to tear your ass in two.

Baby, baby, baby … Just kidding. That's total dogshit! Fucking YouTube tossed it into my "You might like." Fucktards.

I'd love to spit some beechnut in that dude's eye. Shoot him with my old .45.

The pen is the tongue of the mind.

Would you exchange a walk-on part in the war for lead role in a cage?

You sure got a purdy mouth.

I mean, some doctor told me I had six months to live, and I went to his funeral.

They got pearl-handled pistols under their vests. They want me to go out drinking with them tonight.

It is well enough that people of the nation do not understand our banking and monetary system, for if they did, I believe there would be a revolution before tomorrow morning.

And all the years you spent between your birth and death when you thought I should have saved my breath.

Badges? We don't need no stinking badges!

We must reject the idea that every time a law's broken, society is guilty rather than the lawbreaker.

Oh it's the price we gotta pay And all the games we gotta play. Makes me wonder if it's worth it to carry on.

Most people fail in life not because they aim too high and miss but because they aim too low and hit.

It has been my experience that folks who have no vices have very few virtues.

Southern trees bear a strange fruit. Blood on the leaves and blood at the root.

Superman is a hero. But only when his mind is clear. He needs that fix like the rest of us.

Look at me. I'm the one who did this.

I am driven by things I can't explain.

Look what this crazy life is doing to me.

Joke's on those who believe the system's fair.

It ain't easy being green.

You did your best. Life did the rest.

I may be surrounded by a million people, but I still feel all alone.

There's no money in peace.

Some men like the fishin'. Some men like the foulin'. Some men like to hear, to hear the cannonball roaring.

You're not supposed to eat this. You're supposed to bury it.

Road, you gotta take me home.

Which one of you bastards shit in my pants?

It's a hara-kiri knife. Why don't you do us all a favor and break it in?

I believe every day is a gift. It just doesn't have to be socks.

Wake me up inside, before I come undone … Save me from the nothing I've become.

They brought their fucking toys.

Some will live, some will die. Okay, let's just move on.

I may be drunk, but by morning, I'll be sober, and you, my dear, will still be ugly.

Strange how the night moves with autumn closin' in.

Will we ever be set free?

The physician can bury his mistakes, but the architect can only advise his client to plant vines.

You ain't seen what I've seen.

The path that I'm walking I must walk alone.

TEN SHOTS AND FAR BEYOND

In-Th
Vitamin water mixed with grappa should give different results.

T.S.
I found a legit way to write off all my vices, and about twelve people, if I'm lucky, will be reading one of them.

Bulb
It took the coronavirus shutting down the world including Hollywood for CBC (Canadian Broadcasting Corporation) to win an Emmy or Grammy or Oscar or whatever the hell it was. Huh?

????
Eight percent is what God allows, max.

In-Th
That Dave guy on that storage show is proof California needs to wake up.

Bulb
Walking is not exercise unless you're, like, a hundred years old. It's also one of the shittiest forms of transportation only slightly ahead

of those nerd scooters, skateboarding, and riding the bus, but it's not exercising.

Bulb

If you can regurgitate something without effort, it's time for your next album.

LFBF

Why is anyone ever packing at a graveside funeral?

In-Th

I think I just ate dough my wife was saving for tomorrow's breakfast. I'll blame the dogs …

$$$$

Volcano spots—small, flat, fart-like eruptions that can be placed anywhere and controlled with a cell phone app.

In-Th

Hire a dork to fuck with Wikipedia entries just to see how many use it as their voice of reason.

B.M.

Drinking may fuck you long term, but it makes you see the world differently and tolerate family crap for the immediate, so fair enough. We all have to pick our battles.

TFUW

This world is becoming such a mess of tolerance for every idiotic idea. I'm going to create Taco Bell hot sauce shit art. Maybe this should have been under $$$$.

????

Eight to ten hours can be four to six in a pinch.

Bulb

Llamas are kind of a Heinz 57 mix of a small horse, a possible molested sheep, a badass poodle, and an angry six-year-old kid hocking loogies on his little brother.

T.S.

Horror movies often make me smile and laugh. That can't be good.

WTF

Meatless burgers? Mc D's has been serving them for years.

Bulb

Barney was weak and held Fred back. He was purely a coattail-riding follower.

????

Eat chicken only on Wednesdays, only vegetables that start with a Q, B, A, or C on Tuesdays and Thursdays, toss kale in the garbage cart at the grocery store, and have lamb three times per month.

In-Th

I'll bet money that Radar O'Reilly is an angry old man now …

LFBF

If a cow-boy rides a horse, did a Scottish dude come up with riding a sheep?

Bulb

Three a.m. and Roxette both suck. FYI, any hour, Roxette sucks.

T.S.

If I ever went to the bar with someone who ordered a melon liqueur or something with grapefruit in it, I'd likely ditch him there, but inside, I'd want to throat-punch him for being such a dork.

Bulb

Corn is so resilient that it won't change for shit.

????

Is a sprouting fountain just an erupting erection on a statue?

Bulb

If and/or when 26 = 0 more than once in just one sitting, it means it may be time to take at least ten steps ...

WTF

Whoops ... Was that a bird or a toddler?

Bulb

Self-medicating with an $80 bottle of booze is a direct by-product of living soft and not being hungry.

In-Th

Smart and lazy makes you a useless pain in the ass.

Bulb

Whitney's music sucked ten years before the dork in the bedspread pants and metallic vest married her and turned her life into a shit show.

????

Are zombies looking for brains to eat in the movies a secret code about society coming out of Hollywood?

LFBF

Are racists concerned that by the time the coronavirus ends or the next thing hits, we will all be wearing burkas?

Bulb

Timed drinking is stressful and hard ...

WTF
How the fuck were Kevin Dubrow and Terry Dubrow brothers?

B.M.
Deep-end diving boards have the footprints of only the brave and those willing to challenge fear.

In-Th
The UPC numbers are halfway ...

T.S.
The scariest thing that goes bump in the night is me with a glow on trying to turn off the fountain, blow out the tiki torches, and then find my way back to the house door in the dark coming from our grappa shed.

TFUW
"Only the strong survive" has been replaced with "Protect the unwilling."

In-Th
I don't think my male bulldog ever truly forgave me for having his balls chopped off. If I were him, I'd wait until I passed out and kill me.

Bulb
Grappa promotes solid, interesting thoughts until about shot number sixteen. After that, all bets are just lost.

????
Does being left winged and right handed mean you're totally useless?

Bulb
Do people who dot the letter *i* with a happy face think the word *shit* mentally stinks any less?

In-Th

This big fucking spider crawling around my deck is … Nope, was … taunting me.

LFBF

Are Hollywood execs and their hanger-on weirdos the same as the jerk-off, self- righteous politico dickheads with the same insecurity need to control the world?

Bulb

Irony. Blue hair on an eighty-year-old is bad, but when they wore it on their eyes in the eighties, it was hot. Huh?

B.M.

True freedom died with the cavemen.

????

How to become a home decorator—dry rye.

Bulb

Those who like the burn from their booze know that grappa is some-what of a sadist after shot number ten.

In-Th

Damn Wilson's grandkid is a dork …

LFBF

Are hard, stale Cheetos what they grind down to make that cheese sand in boxes of mac and cheese?

TFUW

Days gone by: "I could get hurt doing this. I need to pay attention." Today: "If I get hurt at work, I can get paid and stay home."

T.S.

Leftovers are a drunk's best friend after 2:00 a.m. unless they're in that super-seal Tupperware shit. That crap is harder to get into than a safe at the bank.

LFBF

How was Jesus a Swedish-looking, blond-haired, blue-eyed, non-Viking with a Spanish first name and an English last name born in the Middle East to a married virgin and her 90+-year-old carpenter husband who were walking through the desert? Someone is being less than truthful ...

In-Th

Hypothetically, if a fart turned out to be a shit in my shorts and I tossed them off my deck into Wilson's yard, would anyone know?

WTF

Fucking A&W (a classically iconic Canadian fast-food place) just ran an ad saying that they now use only grass-fed cows for their burgers. What the fuck did they feed them before? BlackBerry phones and newspapers?

Bulb

The easy way usually comes with the most baggage.

In-Th

Pigs flop around in shit but still taste good, but roles reversed has the opposite effect. Huh?

Bulb

"You only live once." Fuckwad! You live every day you're awake (but many take it for granted and just go through yesterday's same motions and don't live at all).

TFUW

Spellcheck automatically changes *fuckwad* to *duckweed*.

T.S.

You have officially made it when you have someone on your payroll to drive, cook for, or protect you.

B.M.

The real world should always have more of a foothold in anyone's soul than the fantasy world does, but it should be on the verge of losing it.

Bulb

Hollywood (the town, not my buddy) couldn't write my life story without fucking it all up.

????

When the fuck did hockey become the boring, gentle cousin to ice dancing? If I could skate, I'd punch the first fucknut dicking around on the ice I could reach and get an $8 million contract for not just using my jock as a place to hide my cell phone and keys. Fucking pussies!

In-Th

It's 2:00 a.m., and my male bulldog keeps snoring so loudly that Fishbelly's lights just came on. Fuck. If he calls the cops, I'm going to end up barfing on their shoes and likely pissing in the back of their squad car ... I better go to bed.

LFBF

Who was the whiskey-filled dipshit who came up with the dork thought that "It's five o'clock somewhere"? With that logic, doesn't it make it any hour anywhere?

T.S.

My inner Jekyll and Hyde come out only after number sixteen, but by then, they're about as dangerous as a toothless geriatric poodle that needs to be carried out into the yard to drop a Hershey biscuit.

Bulb

If Yosemite Sam banged the dog Foghorn Leghorn was always after and they had a love child, it would be the Tasmanian Devil. Ah ha! Code cracked! I figured out the Warner Brothers' little family secrets.

In-Th

Four or five more shots in the hot tub and *Grappa Thoughts* may have come with an obituary.

LFBF

Why is cowshit used as fertilizer and dogshit is a magnet to the waffle on shoes?

????

Self-realization: I have more sticks than baseballs.

LFBF

Do people who cry themselves to sleep do so because they can't afford a shrink, therapy, or quality booze?

Bulb

If there was a competition like the Superbowl called The World's Biggest Retard Award, Dave and Stephen would be up fighting each other for MVP every year for the next decade or so.

B.M.

Memories are like when you pass gas—Some give you a form of comfort while others are just fucking embarrassing.

In-Th

Very few know how to truly take me because I either scare them, intrigue them, or piss them off. But most do remember me.

Bulb

Like most things in life, with grappa, you get what you pay for.

TFUW

Life legends should never come with a net ...

$$$$

A handy hot tub hook on the back of the cover to conveniently hold your towel and bathing suit.

B.M.

Greatness often starts from confusion.

T.S.

People who refuse to take a turn at life's bat are more likely to recognize the back of my head.

WTF

How do single punches in the movies and on TV knock fuckheads out?

????

Does Jollibee's and that falafel place down the road stink less than the barbecued cat in Chicago or other windy cities?

Bulb

FYI, drinking water while getting plowed allows for three to eight more drinks.

LFBF

When the hell did my bulldog sleeping next to me sneak half my bottle of grappa?

TFUW

If smoking kills, could I get my neighbor arrested?

Bulb

Don't fool yourself. Hollywood has the inside scoop on life's shit.

????

This si my nombered eighteened grappa shat and i can still h4dawtting write. Ha!

LFBF

How did Bob Marley get anything done?

In-Th

If I stand up too quickly right now, I might slop on my socks …

Bulb

Some have seen and done too much. Most haven't seen shit and done far too little but claim they have.

LFBF

Where the fuck did my number nine go?

$$$$

Find a dork to build a time machine back to the eighties and sell tickets. Side note to self: Google all the lotto numbers and every championship winner from the decade in every sport, sell stocks in anything that ever brought someone pleasure before 1995, buy a case of good grappa and bury it somewhere to find when we get there, and to overly ensure future retirement protection, buy shares in kale, unusable green energy, shitty music (and the spin-off crap they create, i.e., nauseating perfumes and ugly gym wear), and buy huge blocs of Apple stock and anything our future Martian overlords might like.

Bulb

Spelling matters only when you're sober.

B.M.

I'd bet most New Year's resolutions are broken by the time most go to bed on New Year's Eve.

In-Th

Don't add this to the book, but put those stick cartoons you have been drawing during all the lame webinar classes in the book as well ...

LFBF

Is there DNA in piss? Because my DNA is all over Wilson's side of the fence. Maybe I could just blame it on the dogs. After all, we are the same family ...

Bulb

My male bulldog is so overprotective of us that he barks at big rocks that scare him.

In-Th

My last shot of the night is often dependent on what I have scheduled the next morning ...

Bulb

Within the next dozen years or so, the written word could be used as secret code.

T.S.
I have never been more Canadian than when I walked casually outside in flip-flops, a pair of board shorts, and a toque at twenty-five degrees below zero to jump into my hot tub and have drink in hand as I smoke a Cuban cigar.

In-Th
Maybe I should toss a baked potato with all the fixings on top of the trash for old Russell? I try to do nice things for good people.

WTF
Why am I writing down dumb shit about crappy TV, horrible videos, and embarrassing shit?

????
The bigger the rocks, the deeper the pay.

LFBF
Who's that ugly chick in the Queen video, and why is it about her vacuuming?

In-Th
Yesterday's dork Dungeon Masters and crossword heroes are today's slaves to their jobs.

TFUW
Prediction: 2021–23 are going to be a violent years. (Written November 22, 2020.)

Bulb
Those with an hourless clock figured it out but will always be subject to judgment by those who refuse to.

Bulb

Paranoia is reserved for chickenshits.

B.M.

We are all playing the same game in life, but some keep missing their turns and others are cheating at the wrong stuff.

LFBF

Drinking in the dark next to a farting bulldog is considered pathetic and possibly alcoholism. Drinking in the dark next to a farting bulldog while writing a book of brilliant thoughts and ideas is pure, creative entrepreneurialism.

In-Th

Larger than just living. That should be my mantra …

B.M.

My world works only with me in it.

????

Confusion is the gift that encourages boiled thoughts.

Bulb

"If a tree falls in the forest …" Soon, it will be making the evening news.

Bulb

Mirror, mirror on the wall … You sadistic bitch!

TFUW

Tradition gets questioned, modern thoughts lie, hypnosis creates fear and mistrust, so shot number fourteen and a comfy bed are the last sweet spots we have left.

Bulb
Time makes a fool out of everyone.

In-Th
Fuck me, I promised to do sausage and peppers tomorrow morning for breakfast.

T.S.
Waking up with a rubber bald cap on or a face painted like Bobo the illiterate clown is acceptable only on November 1, and even then, the question "Why the hell did you dress up like a creepy dork clown?" begs to be asked.

LFBF
Do future train wrecks ever see the bent rails they're riding on before they soar off of them?

Bulb
A point of pride with me is that I allow my business to coast to the end of the year only at about 3:30 p.m. on December 31.

T.S.
Never have I ever taken a sick day from anything because I was hungover.

????
Do smelly socks infect stinky shoes, or is it vice versa, and where does athlete's foot fit in?

In-Th
I just got into a karate fight with our Christmas tree, and think I may have killed the elf on a shelf ...

List 7
My Ultimate Dinner/Garden Party Guest List

- Burt Reynolds. Read his tell-all and you'll get it.

- Santana. With the same mindset he had at the original Woodstock

- Alex Trebek

- Robin Williams

- Trudeau Sr. Every party needs a shit disturber.

- The Iron Lady—Maggie Thatcher. Same reason as above.

- Kurt Cobain and his wack-job ex-wife Courtney

- Ozzy Osbourne and his translator. Sitting between Trudeau and Thatcher.

- The Great One and Joey

- The Toxic Twins from their heyday in the seventies

- Lee Majors. He was the fucking *Fall Guy* and once cool as hell when I was, like, nine.

- Cher. She has a huge set of lady balls.

- That Russian leader guy with the ink blot on his head.

- The head Hare Krishna

- Larry Flint

- The Duke. Seated between the previous two.

- Jonah Lomu and the Human Skewer. Two amazing athletes who dominated.

- Sir Edmund Hillary

- Cement head and Lemmy. I had the great fortune of drinking with both of you in days gone by, and you'd both be welcome in my world anytime.

- Churchill. He was a fun drunk.

- Monty Burns. It's a fantasy list, so who cares if he's a cartoon?

- Three-Mile Lyle

- Kid Rock

- Mario Puzo

- Hank Williams Jr. and Sr. and Waylon

- Rodney Dangerfield

- Old Blue Eyes, Sammy, and Dean. The rest of the Rat Pack? Why?

- Genghis Khan. He can do the carving at the politicians' table.

- Patty Hearst

- Pagliacci and Nedda. Every party needs a husband and wife squabbling.

- Hervé Villechaize. Don't be fooled. This guy knew how to live large.

- Bruce Lee

- Elvira

- Russell the garbage man

- Slash

- The painter guy who chopped his ear off.

- Gordon Ramsey and Tony Bourdain. Sitting next to each other and at the table closest to the buffet just for shits and giggles.

- Hemingway

- The original Wonder Woman from TV

- A Neanderthal

- Kim K and her husband Drake. They can sit at the rickety card table behind the shed with whoever brought their kids.

- Sade and Amy Winehouse

- Jordan Belfort

- Attila the Hun

- Slim Whitman. My grandparents used to play his shit all the time, and I'd love to asked him what the hell he was taking when he made those god-awful whistling and yodeling songs. Fucking things still haunt me.

- Joan Jett

- That dork father from the show with the Olsen twins and Uncle Jessie. But not Uncle Jessie or the twins.

- Ronnie Biggs---I want to hear the real story right from the horse's mouth.

- Ray Donovan. It's always good to have someone around who can fix shit when something goes sideways.

- Agatha Christie

- Elvis

- The Blindside Guy. Just to ask him how much more he got his ass kicked after the movie came out.

- Martha Stewart

- Quentin Tarantino. Based purely on his movies, this guy is batshit crazy interesting.

- Nigella Lawson. She is a great chef who should be more famous.

- Reginald Denny and Rodney King

- Stu Hart and the British Bulldog

- Henry Ford

- Michael Jackson's monkey. I'm betting he, she, or it has some stories.

- The three Richards: Branson, Keith, and Little

- The Zodiac Killer
  - Cindi Lauper. I know, but it was starting to look like a total sausage party, and she seems wacky. She can hang with Trudeau Sr. and a couple of the other dipshits I invited for balance.
  - Steven Van Zandt and Ronnie Van Zant
  - Gilbert Gottfried
  - That mumbling rap guy who walks around like he dropped a load in his shorts with the big gold teeth and giant clock around his neck who was banging Sly's ex-wife.
  - Clooney. I got a hunch he might be cool.
  - Mother Teresa
  - Pat Garrett. I want the real story.
  - Don Quixote. The dude had a hard-on for fighting windmills, so he'd likely be pretty damn entertaining.
  - Mike Tyson
  - P. T. Barnum. This guy made a career out of bullshitting. In addition to the circus stuff, he was a politician.
  - Ray Kroc and Harland Sanders
  - Dr. Kavorkian. Sitting next to Mother Teresa because they'd have great dinner conversation I'm sure.
- Gary Larson
- Bocelli
- Rowdy Roddy Piper. One of the last of the world's quality villains.
- Marco Polo. He worked on the actual Silk Road. He must have some stories.
- The My Pillow guy. Anyone that dorky must have some twisted shit in him to talk about and let out.
- The Botched Doctors
- Tawney Kitaen. She banged, like, half of the Hollywood rock scene in the eighties. She must have had some stories.
- Carrot Top. I'm betting he's batshit crazy when you get a few in him.
- Chyna. She was nutbag crazy without question.
- Vincent Price
- Prince and those guys who wore flower pots on their heads in the eighties
- Paul Le Roux
- That prick who watched *Star Trek* so much that it inspired him to create cell phones. I'm inviting him so I can throw potato salad chunks at him all night.

- William Shakespeare. Same reason as above.

- Sarkis Soghanalian. The real Yuri Orlov. This guy knew and did some serious shit.

- Whoever started everyone down the road of political correctness and turned a large portion of the Western world into crybabies. They can be in charge of holding up the target for the drunken archery contest.

- Slowhand

- Santa. Keep him away from the roasted venison and Villechaize.

- Bela Lugosi

- Dominic Chianese

- Michael Richards. This guy got stuck between eras and paid a huge price for it, but he's still funny as hell.

- Cleopatra

- Sam Giancana

- JFK. Seated next to Giancana. They have a lot to talk about and even more in common. Right, Marilyn?

- Don Cheadle

- Shoeless Joe Jackson

- Mr. Hand. I like watching unicorn chasers.

- Lionel Barrymore. Not his boring grandkid.

- Abe Vigoda

- Clint Eastwood

- Chris Isaak

- Alfred Hitchcock

- Evel Knievel and Travis Pastrana

- Walter Payton

- Tony Sirico

- Jack Ma. If you don't know who he is, you will.

My original list included Eddie Van Halen, but I removed him after he passed so it wouldn't look like I was playing off the wave of fanatic, weeping, fan crap. RIP, Ed.

The End

P.S.

B.M.

If anything you do, enjoy doing it. If you enjoy doing it, be the best at it.

ABOUT THE AUTHOR

A self made, world travelled businessman with multiple millions under management, who works very hard all week but enjoys a drink (or several) on the weekends and who doesn't believe in sugar coating life. Bam's built more than 1 successful business in more than 1 country and speaks directly without looking to hurt anyone. In a filtered, sanitized world he's not who'd you'd expect to be writing a book anymore but did in a way you should be demanding from everyone.